PICTURE IT!

A Comprehension Handbook

Author's Purpose

Inform

An author writes for many purposes, some of which are to inform, entertain, persuade, or express a mood or feeling. An author may have more than one purpose for writing.

Entertain

Categorize and Classify

When we categorize and classify, we look at how people or things are related based on their characteristics.

Compare and Contrast

To compare and contrast
is to look for similarities
and differences
in things.

SPEAKS 5 DIFFERENT LANGUAGES

$23.95

•$19.95

ABSOLUTELY NOT PXR201 COMPATIBLE

PXR201 COMPATIBLE

20% OFF!

Draw Conclusions

When we draw conclusions, we think about facts and details and then decide something about them.

Fact and Opinion

A fact is something that can be proved true or false. An opinion can't be proved.

Generalize

To generalize is to make a broad statement or rule that applies to many examples.

Graphic Sources

Graphic sources show information in a way the reader can see.

Table

Tables are boxes, squares, or rectangles that categorize information in rows and columns.

The Case of the
Park Litterbugs

Detective on duty	Day	Garbage found
	Sunday	9
Jaime	Monday	11
Jessica	Tuesday	2
Eric	Wednesday	3
Me	Thursday	5
Ana Luz	Friday	7
Milton	Saturday	15
Libby		

Bar Graph
A bar graph uses horizontal and vertical lines to compare information.

Map
A map is a drawing of a place that shows where something is or where something happened.

Diagram
A diagram is a drawing, usually with parts that are labeled.

PI•11

Room To Grow

Literary Elements

Stories are made up of four main elements: character, setting, plot, and theme. Each of these parts gives you an understanding of the story.

Character

A character is a person or an animal in a story.

Setting

The setting is the time and place in which a story happens.

Plot

The plot is the pattern of events in a story.

The plot starts with a problem or goal and builds toward a climax. The plot ends with a resolution or outcome.

Theme

The theme is the big idea of a story. We look at the plot, setting, or characters to determine the theme of a story.

Main Idea and Details

Main idea is the most important idea about a topic. Details support the main idea.

Sequence

Sequence refers to the order of events in fiction or nonfiction. We also use sequence when we list the steps in a process.

ISBN-13:   978-0-328-63437-8
ISBN-10:   0-328-63437-9
2 3 4 5 6 7 8 9 10 V064 14 13 12 11

PEARSON LANGUAGE CENTRAL

ELD

Consulting Authors

Jim Cummins, Ph.D.

Lily Wong Fillmore, Ph.D.

Georgia García, Ph.D.

Jill Kerper Mora, Ed.D.

PEARSON

Glenview, Illinois • Boston, Massachusetts • Chandler, Arizona •
Upper Saddle River, New Jersey

Unit 1 Turning Points

Unit 2 Teamwork

Question of
the Week

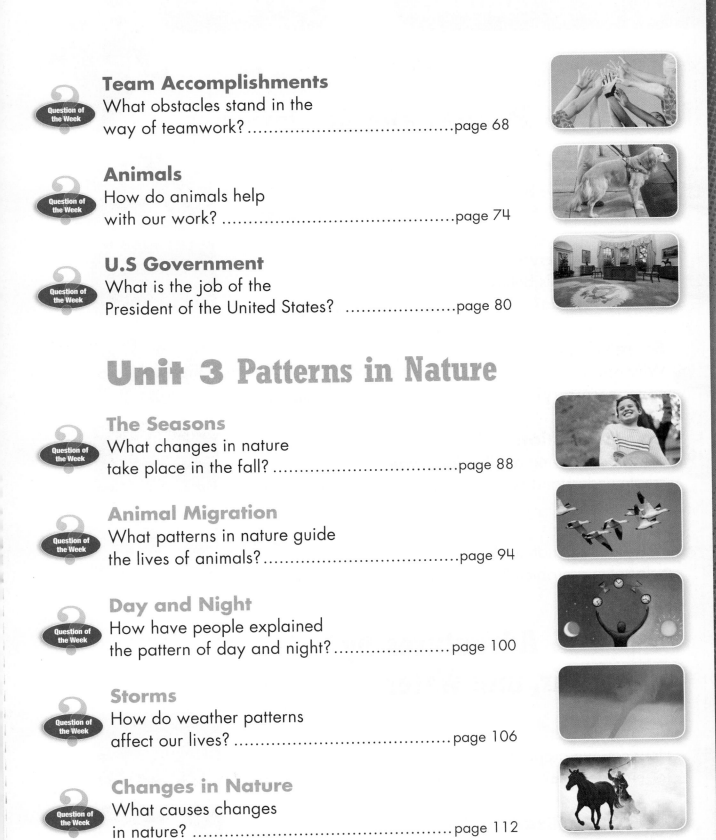

Unit 4 Puzzles and Mysteries

Unit 5 Adventures by Land, Air, and Water

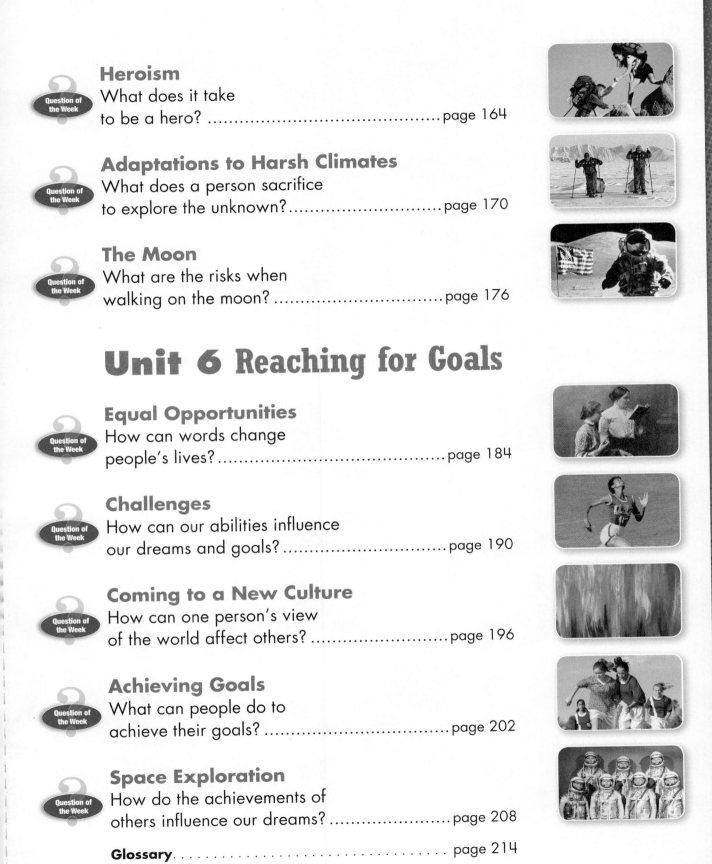

Unit 6 Reaching for Goals

Get
Online!

Hear it!
See it!
Do it!

- Big Question Video
- Concept Talk Video
- Envision It! Animation
- Grammar Jammer

Turning Points

THE BIG ?

What can we discover from new places and people?

Diversity
What experiences bring diverse people together?

Opportunities
What opportunities can be found in new places?

Traveling America
What can we learn about the United States as we travel?

The Southwest
What can we discover in the landscape of the Southwest?

The West
How does Yosemite reflect the unique qualities of the West?

Diversity

Vocabulary

banjo

gourd

parlor

appreciate
culture
diverse
praises

What experiences bring diverse people together?

Making and listening to music brings diverse people together. People from different cultures can appreciate the sounds of an instrument, such as the banjo. They can also enjoy the same type of music.

Read the passage together.
Then circle the vocabulary words.

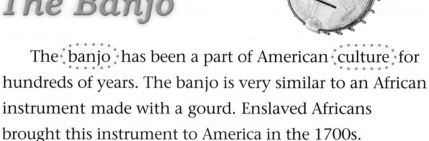

The Banjo

The banjo has been a part of American culture for hundreds of years. The banjo is very similar to an African instrument made with a gourd. Enslaved Africans brought this instrument to America in the 1700s.

By the middle of the 1800s, diverse cultures had begun to appreciate the banjo. Soldiers fighting in the Civil War would relax at night by playing the banjo. After the war, they brought their instruments home.

Women were soon playing the banjo in the parlor of their homes. They usually played for family and friends. The banjo's bright and happy sound won praises from listeners.

Talk About It How did the banjo bring diverse people together? Complete the sentences below.

> The banjo was brought to America by _____.
>
> _____ enjoyed playing the banjo.
>
> Listeners liked the banjo's music because _____.

Your Turn Tell your partner about an instrument you like to play or listen to and why.

I like to [play, listen to] _____ because _____.

Sequencing Sequencing is used to show the order in which things happen. We put the things that happen in a certain order. Words, such as *yesterday* and *today*, can help us tell the order in which things happen.

Example: Hanna spoke to her music teacher **yesterday.**
She will begin her banjo lessons **tomorrow.**

Circle the words that tell when in the sentences below.

yesterday	Juan bought a recording of piano music yesterday.
today	Juan is playing his piano today.
tomorrow	Juan will be ready for school band practice tomorrow.
next week	Next week Juan will learn a new song on the piano.

Talk About It Tell a partner what you did yesterday, what you are doing today, and what you will do tomorrow.

Complete the sentences below.

Yesterday, I _____.

Today, I _____.

Tomorrow, I _____.

Your Turn Write a sentence that tells something you will do tomorrow or next week.

_____

_____

Sequence The order in which things happen in a story is called **sequence.** When you read, it is important to notice the order of events. Look for clue words that tell order such as *first, next, last, yesterday, today,* or *tomorrow.*

A time line is one way to see the sequence of events in a story. This time line shows four days of the week. The sentences below the days tell what happens each day.

Monday

Max practices the violin.

Tuesday

Max brings his violin to school.

Wednesday

Max plays his violin for his class. Tomorrow, he will play for the whole school.

Thursday

Max plays his violin for the whole school. Yesterday, he played for his class.

Talk About It Look at the time line. What is the last thing in the week that Max does? What does he do first? Tell a partner.

Your Turn Read the sentences below. Circle what happened first. Draw a box around what happened last.

Finally, Grace became a music teacher.

First, Grace learned how to play the piano.

Next, Grace learned how to play the banjo.

Interrogative and Declarative Sentences In English, we use different kinds of sentences. A **declarative sentence** tells or explains something. It has a period at the end of the sentence. An **interrogative sentence** asks a question. It has a question mark at the end of the sentence. Look at the examples in the chart below.

Sentences That Tell	Music brings diverse people together.
	It is fun to learn to play the guitar.
	I made friends at my music lesson.
Sentences That Ask	How does music bring people together?
	When will you practice the guitar?
	Can you teach me how to play the flute?

Talk About It Read the sentences. Then circle the end punctuation mark. What kind of sentences are these? Does the sentence tell or ask?

We like to play music.

Do you play an instrument?

Your Turn Read the sentences below. Write in the correct ending punctuation mark.

I went to music practice today

Where did you go

Think, Talk, and Write

Diversity Think about how music brings diverse people together. Talk with a partner about other experiences you could have to bring people together.

How does food bring people together?

How do sports bring people together?

- -

Talk About It Review the vocabulary on page 24. Work with a partner to tell about each word. Which words will you use to write about the experiences that bring diverse people together?

- -

Produce Language Write about an experience you had when people from different cultures came together. First complete the chart. Then write 4 to 5 sentences in your Weekly Concept Journal.

My experience: _____

_____

The diverse people or culture: _____

_____

What I learned: _____

_____

Vocabulary words I can use: _____

_____

Vocabulary

assembly line

conveyor belt

cannery

employment

immigrants

opportunities

promoted

supervisor

wages

What opportunities can be found in new places?

When you go to a new place, there are new opportunities. Many immigrants came to the United States to try to find a better job. In California, many immigrants worked in canneries.

Read the passage together.
Then circle the vocabulary words.

Working in a Cannery

A cannery is a factory where food is prepared and placed in cans. The canneries in San Jose, California, provided employment for thousands of immigrants in the early 1900s.

The process of canning fruit was done on an assembly line. One group of workers would quickly peel the fruit, cut out the pit, and cut it into pieces. When the fruit was prepared, it would move down a conveyor belt to the next group of workers. Those workers would cook the fruit and put it in cans.

A good worker might be promoted and become a supervisor. Supervisors earned higher wages than other workers. Canneries provided many immigrants with great opportunities.

Talk About It What opportunities did immigrants find working in a cannery? Complete the sentences below.

> Workers in a cannery _____ and _____ .
>
> Good workers could be _____ and earn _____ .

Your Turn Think about moving to a new place.
Talk about an opportunity you might find there.
Use the sentence below to help.

When I move to a new place, I might _____ .

Explaining When we explain something, we give more information. We may use adverbs to tell how someone does something.

Example:
> Anna cut the fruit **carefully** and then made sure the pieces were given out **equally.**

We add -*ly* to the end of some words to make new words that tell how something is done.

Circle the words that tell how someone does something in the sentences below.

loudly	Tran banged on the door loudly.
quickly	Alicia worked quickly on the assembly line.
easily	Jorge easily opened the can of fruit for his brother.
proudly	Lin proudly accepted the promotion to supervisor.

Talk About It Think of a sentence that explains how someone does something. Use a word with -*ly*.

Complete the sentences below.

> The workers worked _____ .
>
> Both workers sorted the fruit _____ .

Your Turn Look at the picture. Write a sentence that explains how workers on an assembly line prepare fruit. Use a word with -*ly*.

_____

_____

Author's Purpose An author usually has one or more reasons for writing. These reasons are the **author's purpose.** Writers may use special words depending on the purpose. For example, a writer may use words that end with *-ly* to explain how something is done.

Express
wants reader to feel something

Persuade
convince reader to think in a certain way

Reasons for Writing

Entertain
wants reader to enjoy text

Inform
gives reader information

Talk About It Have you ever read a funny story? What was the author's purpose? What is the author's purpose in a news article? Complete the sentences with a partner.

In a funny story, the writer _____.

In a news article, the writer _____.

The purposes are different because _____.

Your Turn Reread the passage on page 31. What do you think the author's purpose was for writing the passage? Explain why.

_____

_____

Imperative and Exclamatory Sentences In English, we use different kinds of sentences. An **imperative sentence** tells someone to do something. It has a period at the end of the sentence. An **exclamatory sentence** shows a strong feeling. It has an exclamation point at the end of the sentence.

Imperative Sentences that tell someone to do something	Come here.
	Go to work.
	Please help me do this.
Exclamatory Sentences that show strong feeling	I love working here!
	You did a great job!
	Wow! That's fantastic!

Talk About It Read the sentences. Then circle the end punctuation mark. What kind of sentences are these? Does the sentence tell someone to do something or show strong feeling?

Look at the drawing.

I just got promoted!

Your Turn Write one imperative sentence and one exclamatory sentence. Use the words below to help you.

job   find   factory   see   broken   start   turn

_____

_____

Think, Talk, and Write

Opportunities Think about how immigrants in the 1900s had opportunities to earn money by working in canneries. Talk with a partner about other opportunities for employment that people have today.

Is building houses
a good opportunity?

Is working with computers
a good opportunity?

Talk About It Review the vocabulary on page 30. Work with a partner to tell about each word. Which words will you use to write about the opportunities you can find in new places?

Produce Language Write about an opportunity that immigrants have today. First complete the chart. Then write 4 to 5 sentences in your Weekly Concept Journal.

Job opportunity: _____

_____

Why it is a good opportunity: _____

_____

How people can find this opportunity: _____

_____

Vocabulary words I can use: _____

_____

PICTURE IT! cliffs

PICTURE IT! highway

PICTURE IT! plains

countless
longed
towering

What can we learn about the United States as we travel?

Many people travel around the United States by car. They get to see and learn more about our country. Some of these roads, such as historic Route 66, played important roles in U.S. history.

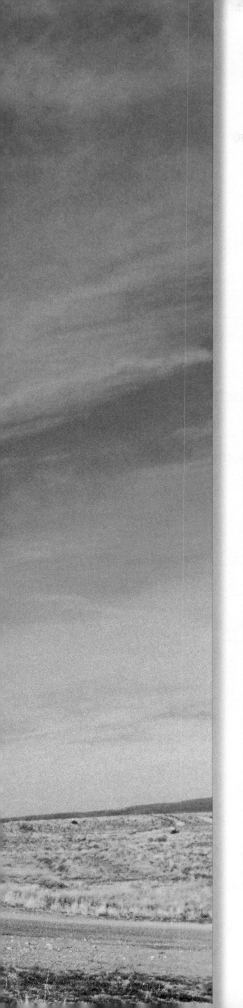

Read the passage together.
Then circle the vocabulary words.

Traveling on Route 66

From the 1920s through the 1960s, countless Americans were traveling on Route 66. This two-lane highway was the shortest route from Chicago, Illinois, to Los Angeles, California. It spanned about 2,400 miles and cut through eight states. Travelers on the road drove through America's Great Plains and deserts. They saw steep cliffs towering in the distance.

This road was very important during the Great Depression of the 1930s. Thousands of people who were out of work traveled Route 66. They longed for jobs and new lives in California. Route 66 became a symbol of their hope.

This highway was so important, in fact, that it was called the "Mother Road" and the "Main Street of America." You can still travel parts of Route 66 today.

Talk About It What can people learn about the United States by knowing about Route 66? Complete the sentences below.

> In the mid-1900s, _____ was the shortest way to get from _____ to _____.
>
> Travelers on Route 66 could learn about America's land by seeing _____ and _____.

Your Turn What are some reasons people might have traveled on Route 66? Tell your partner.

Sequencing We use certain words that help us tell things in the order in which they happened. These words answer the question *when?*

Example:

> The family could not leave for their trip **until** their suitcases were put in the car.

Circle the words that answer the question *when?* in the sentences below.

until	The family traveling on Route 66 did not want to take a break until they reached Missouri.
before	The family had to travel through Oklahoma before they could reach Texas.
after	They reached Los Angeles after traveling through eight states.

Talk About It Look at the map of Route 66. Say sentences about traveling from Chicago to Los Angeles. Use *before* and *after*.

Complete the sentences with a partner.

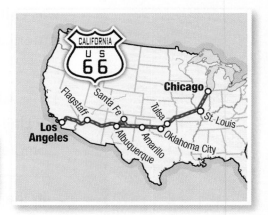

> I traveled through St. Louis _____ Tulsa.
>
> I traveled through Santa Fe _____ Tulsa.

Your Turn Write a sentence about traveling on Route 66. Use a word that answers the question *when?*

_____

_____

Sequence The order in which things happen is called **sequence.** When you read, it is important to notice the sequence of events. Look for words that answer the question *when?* to help you determine the sequence of events.

First, my family planned our trip along Route 66. Then we packed, and my mom and dad loaded our suitcases into the car. After loading our suitcases, we started our trip along the highway. We passed through three states before getting to California. Finally, we arrived in Los Angeles, California.

· ·

Talk About It Read the paragraph above. Retell what happened in sequence. Use words that answer the question *when?*

Complete the sentences below with a partner.

After they _____ , the family _____ .

Before getting to California, they _____ .

Finally, they _____ .

· ·

Your Turn Look at the pictures of the family traveling to Los Angeles. Put the pictures in the correct sequence. Number them *1, 2,* and *3.*

_____   _____   _____

Grammar

Subjects and Predicates A complete sentence in English has a **subject** and a **predicate.** The subject is who or what the sentence is about. The predicate tells something about the subject.

Subject	Predicate
Luis	rides in the car.
The people	like to travel.
California	is a western state.
Students	read about Route 66.
The class	is studying about the United States.
The family	likes to sing in the car.

Talk About It What are the subjects in these sentences? Discuss your answers with a partner.

Route 66 is a two-lane highway.

Countless cars have traveled on Route 66.

People traveled on Route 66 for many years.

Your Turn Circle the subject in each sentence. Underline the predicate.

California is a beautiful place to visit.

Route 66 is about 2,400 miles long.

My family and I drove on Route 66.

Think, Talk, and Write

Traveling America Think about the different things people might have seen as they traveled on Route 66 during the 1900s. Talk with a partner about other places you can travel to in the United States.

Many people travel to the beach in California.

Many people travel to the Grand Canyon.

- -

Talk About It Review the vocabulary on page 36. Work with a partner to tell about each word. Which words will you use to write about what you can learn about the United States as you travel?

- -

Produce Language Write about the things you have learned or might learn as you travel. First complete the chart. Then write 4 to 5 sentences in your Weekly Concept Journal.

Where I traveled or want to travel: _____

_____

Things I did see or might see: _____

_____

Details about what I saw: _____

_____

Vocabulary words I can use: _____

_____

Vocabulary

cactus

desert

roadrunner

tortoise

harsh

landscape

riverbed

What can we discover in the landscape of the Southwest?

Many people visit the American Southwest to see the beautiful landscape. America's great deserts are in the Southwest.

Read the passage together.
Then circle the vocabulary words.

The Deserts of the Southwest

The deserts of the American Southwest are hot and dry. During the daytime, temperatures can go above 100 degrees. The deserts also get very little rain.

Although the deserts of the Southwest are harsh places, many plants and animals are able to live there. In the desert, you might see a roadrunner, a tortoise, a bobcat, or a lizard. Cattle can live in the desert too. Large cactus plants and some trees and shrubs are also found in the desert.

Many people travel to the deserts of the American Southwest to take in the beauty of the landscape. There, they see huge cliffs, winding riverbeds, and interesting plants and animals.

• •

Talk About It What interesting things can be discovered by visiting the Southwest? Complete the sentences below.

The deserts of the Southwest are _____ .

Many animals, such as lizards, _____ , and _____ , live in the deserts.

The landscape of the deserts includes _____ .

• •

Your Turn Look at the main picture. Would you like to visit the deserts of the Southwest? Why or why not? Tell a partner.

Interpreting People use words to tell how they feel or what they think about something. They may use special language to show that they feel strongly about something.

Example: The Southwest is the **best** place in the United States. Everyone **should** visit the Southwest.

Read the sentences below. Circle the words and phrases that show strong feelings.

best	My trip to the Arizona desert was the best vacation I have ever had.
should	We should all visit the Southwest.
worst	My trip to the Arizona desert was the worst vacation I have ever taken.
should not	You should not visit the Southwest.

Talk About It Look at the two pictures below. Choose which place you like better. Say a sentence that shows you feel strongly about this place.

Grand Canyon

Joshua Tree National Park

Your Turn Write a sentence about one of the places above. Use words that show you feel strongly about this place.

_____

_____

Author's Purpose An author has one or more reasons for writing something. These reasons are the **author's purpose.** Authors write to persuade, or to try and get you to think or act in a certain way. Authors also write to inform, or to explain something. They also write to entertain or to express an idea.

You should visit the deserts of the Southwest! There is no more beautiful place in the United States than the deserts of the Southwest. You will love the beauty of the land, and you will see amazing plants and animals. It will be one of the best vacations you will ever have.

Talk About It Read the short passage above. What is the author's purpose? How do you know? Complete the sentences below with a partner.

The author wrote the passage to _____ .

The author wants people to _____ .

Your Turn Reread the passage on page 43. What was the author's purpose? Explain why.

_____

_____

Compound Sentences A sentence that joins two simple sentences is called a **compound sentence.** Compound sentences use a word, called a coordinating conjunction, to join the two simple sentences. Most compound sentences use a comma before the joining word.

Examples of Compound Sentences	Coordinator
Roadrunners live in the desert, **and** they can run very fast.	**and**
Many people travel to the Southwest, **for** it is very beautiful there.	**for**
I live in California, **but** my cousins live near the desert in Arizona.	**but**
We can go to the Grand Canyon, **or** we can hike in the desert.	**or**
It took a long time to go through the desert, **yet** it seemed like a short trip.	**yet**
There is little rainfall in Southwestern deserts, **so** the soil is very dry.	**so**

Talk About It Read these sentences and decide which ones are compound sentences. Explain why you think so.

Hiking in the desert is fun, yet it can also be dangerous.

My family took a vacation in New Mexico and Arizona.

The desert can be very hot, but it can also be very beautiful.

Your Turn Join the sentences below to make a compound sentence. Use a coordinator from the chart.

I like to visit the desert, _____ I don't like it when it's hot.

We can go to Texas, _____ we can go to Arizona.

Think, Talk, and Write

The Southwest Think about the plants and animals that live in America's Southwest. Talk with a partner about other animals and plants that live in the desert.

Do snakes live in the desert?

Do flowers grow in the desert?

Talk About It Review the vocabulary on page 42. Work with a partner to tell about each word. Which words will you use to write about the Southwest landscape?

Produce Language Write about an animal or plant that lives in the desert. First complete the chart. Then write 4 to 5 sentences in your Weekly Concept Journal.

My animal or plant: _____

_____

What desert it lives in: _____

_____

What my animal eats or how the plant gets water: _____

_____

Vocabulary words I can use: _____

_____

Vocabulary

PICTURE IT!

habitat

PICTURE IT!

meadow

PICTURE IT!

sequoia

PICTURE IT!

waterfall

impressive
preserve
shelter
unique
wilderness

How does Yosemite reflect the unique qualities of the West?

Yosemite National Park was one of the first wilderness parks in the United States. The land in Yosemite has unique qualities of the West. Thousands of plants and animals live in Yosemite.

Read the passage together.
Then circle the vocabulary words.

Yosemite National Park

Yosemite National Park is an impressive place to visit. If you visit, you might see a huge waterfall, mountains, or a peaceful meadow. Yosemite also has forests and thousands of lakes and ponds. Some giant sequoia trees can be found in the park. These kinds of trees are unique to the West.

Unlike some other state parks, almost all of Yosemite is a true wilderness preserve. The park is famous for its different habitats. Each protected habitat provides food and shelter for many different kinds of animals. Black bears, beavers, and great gray owls are some of the many animals that are protected in the park.

Talk About It What are some unique qualities of Yosemite National Park? Complete the sentences below.

Yosemite has huge waterfalls, _____, _____, and _____.

Almost all of Yosemite is a wilderness _____ and provides _____ for many different kinds of animals.

Your Turn Look at the picture of Yosemite. What are some unique characteristics of the park? Tell your partner.

Summarizing We **summarize** what something is mostly about using only a few words. We can use words, such as *so* and *and*, to join together ideas that help tell the main point.

Example: Insects like to live in meadows, **so** insect-eating Yosemite toads also like to live there.

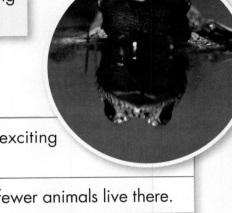

Circle the word in each sentence that joins together the ideas in the sentences below.

and	Yosemite is almost entirely wilderness, and it is an exciting place for people to visit.
	The rocky areas of Yosemite have fewer plants, and fewer animals live there.
so	Yosemite National Park is popular, so large parking lots are needed.
	Yosemite is a protected park, so many animals are able to survive there.

Talk About It Look at the picture. Say a sentence that tells what the picture is about. Use a word from the chart above that joins together your ideas.

Complete the sentences with a partner.

> Yosemite _____ , and _____ .
>
> Yosemite is _____ , so _____ .

Your Turn Write a sentence that tells the main point in the picture above. Use *and* or *so* in your sentence.

_____

_____

Main Idea and Details Every piece of writing has a **main idea** and **details** that support the main idea. The main idea is what the writing is mostly about.

Many animals live in the meadows in Yosemite National Park. The meadows have plenty of fresh water and food. Beavers and great grey owls live in the meadows. Insects like to live in meadows, so insect-eating Yosemite toads also like to live there.

Talk About It What is the main idea of the paragraph? What are some details that tell more about the main idea?

Complete the sentences with a partner.

> The main idea is that many animals _____ .
>
> One detail is _____ .
>
> Another detail is _____ .

Your Turn Read the following paragraph. Write the main idea. Then identify three supporting details.

California is located in the western United States. It is the third-largest state in the United States. It covers more than 163,000 square miles. The California coast is 840 miles long. It has many tall mountains.

_____

_____

Clauses and Complex Sentences A **clause** is a group of words that has a subject and a verb. A clause that can stand alone as a sentence is an **independent clause.** A clause that cannot stand alone as a sentence is a **subordinate**, or dependent, **clause.** A **complex sentence** is formed when an independent clause is joined with a subordinate clause.

Examples of Complex Sentences	Words That Join Clauses
Visitors enjoy Yosemite National Park because they can see many different things there.	**because**
Gold was found in the Sierra Nevada, which is how many people came to know about Yosemite.	**which**
Naturalists asked the government to protect Yosemite when they discovered the many habitats there.	**when**

Talk About It Read each sentence. What are the independent clauses? What are the subordinate clauses? Circle the words that join two clauses together to make a complex sentence.

Photographers couldn't wait to start taking pictures when they saw Yosemite's sights.

Beavers like to live where the meadow and forest meet because they can find food and shelter there.

Your Turn Complete the sentence below to make a complex sentence.

When I visit Yosemite, I _____ .

52

Think, Talk, and Write

The West Think about Yosemite National Park. Talk with a partner about what makes Yosemite unique to the West.

How is Vernal Falls unique?

How is Mount Watkins unique?

- -

Talk About It Review the vocabulary on page 48. Work with a partner to tell about each word. Which words will you use to write about how Yosemite reflects the unique qualities of the West?

- -

Produce Language Write about an animal, plant, or place in Yosemite, such as a waterfall. Tell what makes it unique. First complete the chart. Then write 4 to 5 sentences in your Weekly Concept Journal.

My unique animal, plant, or place: _____

_____

Why it is unique: _____

_____

Vocabulary words I can use: _____

_____

Get Online!

Hear it!
See it!
Do it!

- Big Question Video
- Concept Talk Video
- Envision It! Animation
- Grammar Jammer

Teamwork

THE BIG ? What is the value of teamwork?

Developing New Understandings
How can we learn to appreciate the talents of others?

Working Together
How can we work together to achieve a goal?

Team Accomplishments
What obstacles stand in the way of teamwork?

Animals
How do animals help with our work?

U.S. Government
What is the job of the President of the United States?

Teamwork

Vocabulary

PICTURE IT!

KENYA
380

KENYA
382

athletes

PICTURE IT!

11   17

uniforms

compete
fouled
talent
unbelievable

How can we learn to appreciate the talents of others?

Everyone has things they can do well. People can have many different talents. Some paint beautiful pictures. Some can sing well. Others might be athletes who are good at certain sports. We can appreciate these different talents by thanking others for the things they do well.

Vocabulary in Context

Read the passage together.
Then circle the vocabulary words.

The Basketball Game

It was the first basketball game of the year. A crowd of people sat around the basketball court. They were ready to watch the game.

The teams came onto the court. The Tigers wore green uniforms. The Wildcats wore red uniforms. They were ready to compete!

The crowd cheered because a player made a basket. The crowd yelled because a player was fouled. The game was tied with five seconds left. Then a Wildcat made a basket. It was an unbelievable shot!

The crowd stood up and cheered. The Wildcats won. It was easy to appreciate these athletes. They had a lot of talent!

. . . .

Talk About It What happened at the basketball game? Complete the sentences below.

The crowd of people _____ .

The Wildcats _____ .

. . . .

Your Turn Think of a classmate who has a talent. How do you appreciate this talent? Complete the sentences below.

_____ is good at _____ .

I can appreciate the talent by _____ .

57

Language Workshop

Cause-and-Effect Relationship We use words to write about things that happen. In a sentence, an **effect** is what happens. A **cause** is why it happens. Sometimes clue words come before or after causes and effects.

Example: The crowd got excited **because** the player scored two points.

Because is a clue word. The words after *because* tell the cause: What happened? The crowd got excited. The words before *because* tell the effect: Why did it happen? The player scored two points.

Circle the clue words in each sentence.
Then underline the words that show causes.

Clue Words	Sentences
because	We went to the gym because there was a game.
so that	We cheered loudly so that our team would know we cared.
as a result	Our team won. As a result, we were very happy.
for this reason	The other team tried hard. For this reason, we clapped for them too.

Talk About It Use clue words that make sense in each sentence below.

We clapped for Benny _____ he ran faster than everyone else.

Daniel gets good grades in school. _____, his parents are proud of him.

Your Turn Think of something that happened today. Tell about why it happened. Use the clue word *because* in your sentence.

_____ because _____.

Cause and Effect We often read about things that happened and why they happened. A **cause** is why something happened. An **effect** is what happened.

Sometimes a sentence has clue words to help you find causes and effects. Other times there are no clue words.

Example:
> Team A won the game **because** they scored more points.

In this example, *because* is the clue word. *They scored more points* is the cause. It tells the reason why Team A won the game. *Team A won the game* is the effect.

Talk About It Read the sentences. What is the cause? What is the effect?

Complete the chart with a partner.

> The team won the game.
> As a result, the team got a medal.

CAUSE:		EFFECT:
_____		_____
_____		_____

Your Turn Read the passage on page 57. Underline a cause. Circle an effect.

Grammar

Common and Proper Nouns A **common noun** names any person, place, or thing. It begins with a lowercase letter, such as *a*, *b*, or *c*. A **proper noun** names a specific person, place, or thing, such as a town. It needs a capital letter, such as *A*, *B*, or *C*. The common and proper nouns are circled in the chart below.

Common Nouns	Proper Nouns
The (team) played in that (city).	The (Bulldogs) played in (Cedarville).
The (athletes) competed in the (games).	(Jeff) and (Lionel) competed in the (Special Olympics).

Talk About It Read the sentences. Circle the common nouns. Underline the proper nouns.

The athletes came from Arizona.

Uncle Jim clapped louder than his dad.

Sara felt proud of her teammates.

Your Turn Write a common or proper noun in each sentence. Then write a sentence of your own.

(common noun) We cheered for the _____.

(proper noun) _____ will try out for the team.

_____

_____

Think, Talk, and Write

Developing New Understandings Think about how the crowd appreciated the athletic talent of the Wildcats basketball team. Talk with a partner about ways you can show that you appreciate others.

How do I show that I appreciate my teacher?

How do I show that I appreciate music?

Talk About It Review the vocabulary on page 56. Work with a partner to tell about each word. Which words will you use to write about appreciating the talents of others?

Produce Language Write a letter telling someone that you appreciate his or her talent. First complete the chart. Then write 4 to 5 sentences in your Weekly Concept Journal.

The person's name: _____

_____

The person's talent: _____

_____

The reason you appreciate him or her: _____

_____

Vocabulary words I can use: _____

_____

Vocabulary

coyote

herd

ranch

achieve
distance
relieved
strayed

How can we work together to achieve a goal?

People all across the world work together to achieve goals. A goal may be small, like making lunch for friends. A goal may also be difficult, like saving sheep that escaped from a pen.

Vocabulary in Context

Read the passage together.
Then circle the vocabulary words.

The Roundup

Early morning is usually a quiet time at our ranch. Today was different. The sheep herd was gone when the other ranchers and I arrived at their pen. The sheep had escaped during the night. We heard a coyote in the distance. We knew that to achieve our goal of saving the sheep from the coyote, we had to work together.

Some sheep were still nearby. Other sheep strayed, but we did not know how far. We split up to look for the stray sheep. We were relieved when we found them all safe.

We could not have done the job without working together. Even our border collie, Sam, helped out this time!

Talk About It How did working together help the ranchers achieve a goal? Complete the sentences below.

When the ranchers arrived at the pen, the sheep were _____ .

The ranchers needed to find the sheep because _____ .

By _____ , the ranchers finally found all of the sheep.

Your Turn Think about other ways people might work together on a farm or ranch. Tell a partner.

Language Workshop

Draw Conclusions A conclusion is a decision you make when you think about facts and details. We draw conclusions when we compare things. We can use *-er* words to compare.

Example: The dog is **smaller** than the sheep.

The word *smaller* is an *-er* word.
It compares the size of things.

Circle the *-er* word in each sentence below.
The first one is done for you.

> Blackie is slower than Smoke.
>
> The coyote is bigger than the dog.
>
> The sheep are safer inside the corral.

Talk About It Say a sentence about the picture. Use an *-er* word to compare the sheep.

Your Turn Write a sentence to compare these animals. Use an *-er* word in your sentence.

_____

_____

Draw Conclusions To **draw conclusions,** you use what you already know and details you read or see to make decisions.

Sometimes an *-er* word helps us draw a conclusion. Sometimes our conclusion includes a word with *-er*. Sometimes there are no *-er* words.

Circle the *-er* words in the chart.

Details from Text	Conclusions
The roundup was quicker this time.	The roundup last time was slower.
The ranchers missed breakfast because they woke up at 7:00 A.M.	Breakfast is served before 7:00 A.M.
It takes one hour to round up the cattle. It takes two hours to round up the sheep.	It is harder to round up the sheep.

Talk About It Look at the story on page 63. What conclusions can you draw?

Complete the sentences below with a partner.

Ranchers worry about coyotes because coyotes _____ .

The ranchers found all of the sheep. The ranchers _____ .

Your Turn Look at the story on page 63. Write a conclusion about the border collie Sam. Use an *-er* word in your sentence.

_____

_____

_____

Regular Plural Nouns A **plural noun** names more than one person, place, or thing. In English we often add -s to nouns to make them plural. Nouns that end in the letters s, ch, sh, x, or z need -es added to them instead.

Noun	Plural Noun	Sentence with Plural Noun
horse + s	horses	The horses grazed.
dog + s	dogs	The dogs helped us with the roundup.
ranch + es	ranches	The ranches are in the mountains.

Talk About It Make each word plural. Then use the plural word to complete the sentence.

(rancher) The _____ woke up early.

(coyote) We heard _____ in the distance.

(ranch) The _____ are very large.

Your Turn Write the plural form of each noun below. Then write a sentence using the plural noun.

Singular Noun	Plural Noun	Sentence with Plural Noun
corral		
bush		
field		

Think, Talk, and Write

Working Together Think about how the ranchers worked together to save the sheep from escaping the pen. Talk with a partner about how you achieved a goal by working with others.

How can people work together to grow a garden?

How can people work together to make lunch?

Talk About It Review the vocabulary on page 62. Work with a partner to tell about each word. Which words will you use to write about a goal you achieved?

Produce Language Write about how you achieved a goal by working together with others. First complete the chart. Then write 4 to 5 sentences in your Weekly Concept Journal.

My goal: _____

_____

People who helped: _____

_____

The steps we took: _____

_____

Vocabulary words I can use: _____

_____

Vocabulary

argument

expensive

arrangements

discovered

fundraiser

obstacle

raised

teamwork

What obstacles stand in the way of teamwork?

People can get a lot of work done if they get along. But people may have different ideas about what needs to be done. They may also disagree on what should be done in the first place.

Read the passage together.
Then circle the vocabulary words.

The Problem

The soccer team wanted to go to camp this summer. But first they had to face an (obstacle). Camp was (expensive). So the team decided to have a fundraiser.

Some team members wanted to have a car wash. Others wanted to sell T-shirts. The team had an argument about which fundraiser was better. Then the team discovered that they could have both fundraisers. The team had to work twice as hard, but they knew it would be worth it.

In the end, they raised enough money for camp. The coach called to make arrangements for the team to go to camp. It could not have happened without teamwork!

Talk About It What were the obstacles in the story? Complete the sentences below.

> The team did not _____.
>
> The team argued because _____.

Your Turn Two students need to write a report together. What obstacle do they have? How do they solve their problem?

The students' obstacle is _____.

They can solve their problem by _____.

Draw Conclusions A conclusion is a decision you make about things you see or read.

Words such as *although*, *because*, and *that* can help you tell why you made your conclusions. The sentences in the chart are conclusions about the text on page 69.

Helping Words	Conclusions
although	(Although) the team argued, they still wanted to raise money together.
because	(Because) the team had two fundraisers, they probably made more money than they needed.
that	The team's hard work toward fundraising probably means (that) they work hard when they play soccer too.

Talk About It Complete each sentence with *although*, *because*, or *that*.

_____ they did not agree, they could not get to work right away.

_____ it meant more work, the team decided to have both fundraisers.

Having two fundraisers means _____ the team will make more money.

Your Turn Write why you think the team wanted to go to camp. Use *although*, *because*, or *that* in your sentence.

_____

_____

Drawing Conclusions Readers think about details as they read a text. Readers use these details to **draw conclusions.**

Example:

Detail:
The team worked together all day. Sometimes they disagreed, but they finished what they had to do.

Conclusion:
Although the team disagreed at times, the team worked well together.

Talk About It Read the sentences below.
Use the details to draw a conclusion with your partner.
Use *although*, *because*, or *that* in your conclusion.

Walter was excited about the art fair.

He thought he might win this year.

Your Turn Draw a conclusion about the passage on page 69.
Use the sentence frame to help you.

The students were _____ because _____.

Grammar

Irregular Plural Nouns A plural noun names more than one person, place, or thing. Most plural nouns end with *-s* or *-es*. **Irregular plural nouns** are different. Some irregular plural nouns are listed in the chart below.

Singular Noun	Plural Noun	Sentence with Plural Noun
mouse 	mice 	The **mice** ran around everywhere.
child 	children 	The **children** played soccer on a team.
woman 	women 	The **women** held a fundraiser.

Talk About It Read the sentences and circle the irregular plural nouns. Then say the singular form of each noun.

> The children raised money for camp.
>
> The mice have long tails.

Your Turn Finish the sentence. Use irregular plural nouns from the chart.

The _____ asked the _____ to help them.

Think, Talk, and Write

Team Accomplishments Think about how the soccer team used teamwork to raise money for camp. Talk with a partner about how a group can use teamwork to face their obstacles.

How do mountain climbers work together?

How does a family work together?

Talk About It Review the vocabulary on page 68. Work with a partner to tell about each word. Which words will you use to write about a group that used teamwork to accomplish a goal?

Produce Language Write about how a team used teamwork to accomplish a goal. First complete the chart. Then write 4 to 5 sentences in your Weekly Concept Journal.

My team: _____

_____

My team's obstacle: _____

_____

My team's goal: _____

_____

Vocabulary words I can use: _____

_____

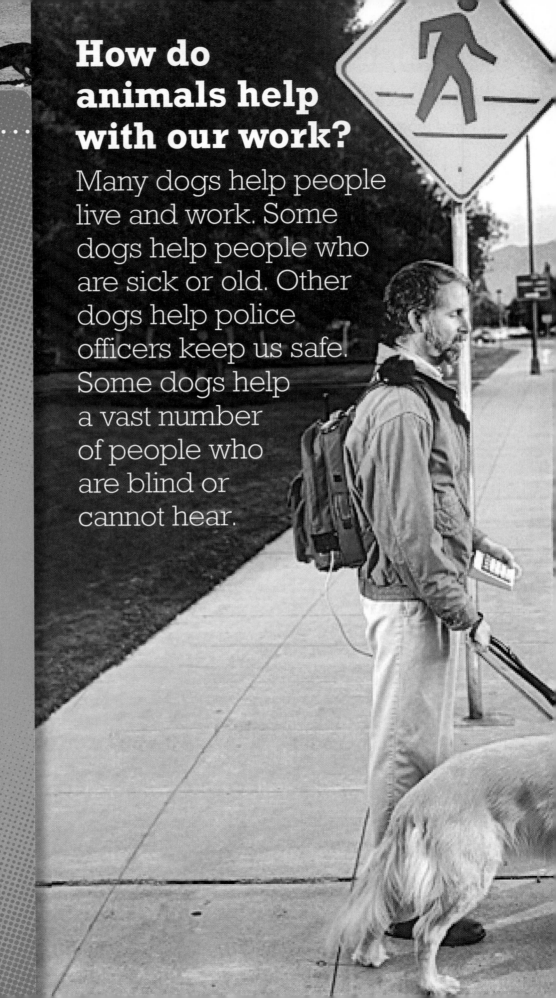

Vocabulary

service dog

transportation

blind
independent
rickety
training
vast

How do animals help with our work?

Many dogs help people live and work. Some dogs help people who are sick or old. Other dogs help police officers keep us safe. Some dogs help a vast number of people who are blind or cannot hear.

Read the passage together.
Then circle the vocabulary words.

Guide Dogs

A service dog helps people live and work. Guide dogs are one kind of service dog. They help blind people lead independent lives.

Guide dogs get special training. They must pass many tests before they can guide blind people. They learn how to be a blind person's "eyes." They help blind people cross streets and climb stairs. They can warn blind people about cars coming or other things they see. They can warn about obstacles or dangers, such as rickety steps.

Service dogs can go to many places. They can go wherever blind people go. They can go into museums and restaurants. They are allowed on all kinds of transportation, even airplanes.

For many blind people, dogs are also good friends. They help keep blind people safe and happy. As one blind person said, "Guide dogs are the best dogs in the world."

Talk About It How do service dogs help blind people? Complete the sentences below.

Service dogs _____ .

Service dogs can go _____ .

Your Turn What do you think is best about guide dogs? Why? Tell your ideas to a partner.

FORM & FUNCTION

Expressing and Supporting Opinions An opinion is something we think. It may not be something that others agree with. We support our opinions with reasons and information. We often tell our opinions by using words such as *in my opinion*. We can use words such as *because* to explain why we think our opinion is right.

Example: **In my opinion,** service dogs are better than normal pets **because** they are so helpful.

Clue Words	Opinions
I think that...because	I think that I would like to train service dogs because it would be fun.
I believe that...since	I believe that we should get Marta a service dog since she is now blind.
In my opinion...so	In my opinion, service dogs should get a lot of treats so they know how important they are.

Talk About It Say a sentence that expresses and supports your opinion about service dogs. Use clue words from above in your sentence.

I think that _____ because _____ .

Your Turn Write a sentence that expresses and supports an opinion about the horse.

_____

_____

Fact and Opinion A **fact** is a statement we can prove is true. An **opinion** is a person's idea that cannot be proven true. Opinions can be disagreed with. Read examples of facts and opinions below. Notice that some, but not all, opinions use clue words such as *I think*.

Facts	Opinions
Service dogs are allowed in restaurants.	I think that some cats should be allowed in restaurants because some dogs are allowed.
Long ago horses pulled covered wagons.	It would be fun to ride in a covered wagon.
Some people use cats to catch mice.	I believe that mice are cute, so we should keep them away from cats.

Talk About It Which sentences below are facts? Which are opinions? Talk about why each sentence is a fact or opinion with a partner. Circle the facts. Underline the opinions.

Some dogs visit hospitals. Their job is to try to make people happy. These dogs are called therapy dogs. In my opinion, all hospitals should have therapy dogs.

Your Turn Look at the passage on page 75. Write one fact from the passage. Write one opinion from the passage.

Singular Possessive Nouns Possessive nouns show ownership. A **singular possessive noun** shows that something belongs to one person or thing. A singular possessive noun uses 's to show belonging. The singular possessive nouns are circled in the sentences below.

Singular Noun	Singular Possessive Noun	Sentence	Explanation
Sonya	Sonya's	Sonya's dog helps her get to work.	The dog belongs to Sonya.
dog	dog's	The dog's leash is on the table.	The leash belongs to the dog.
bus	bus's	The dog climbed up the bus's stairs.	The stairs belong to the bus.

Talk About It Read the first sentence and circle the singular possessive noun. Complete the second sentence by explaining what belongs to someone or something else.

The dog's bowl is full of water.

The _____ belongs to _____ .

Your Turn Write three sentences using the following singular possessive nouns.

(police officer's) _____

_____

(horse's) _____

_____

(boy's) _____

_____

Think, Talk, and Write

Animals Think about how guide dogs help blind people go places and keep them from danger. Talk with a partner about other dogs that help people work.

How do dogs help the police?

How do dogs help ranchers?

Talk About It Review the vocabulary on page 74. Work with a partner to tell about each word. Which words will you use to write about an animal and how it provides help to others?

Produce Language Write a report about an animal and how it helps others work. First complete the chart. Then write 4 to 5 sentences in your Weekly Concept Journal.

My animal: _____

My animal's job: _____

_____

How my animal helps: _____

_____

Vocabulary words I can use: _____

_____

Vocabulary

citizens

White House

decisions
government
politics
responsibility
seriously
speeches

What is the job of the President of the United States?

The citizens of the United States vote for the leader of their country, called the President. The President has a responsibility to help and lead Americans.

Read the passage together.
Then circle the vocabulary words.

THE JOB OF THE PRESIDENT

The President is the head of the government of the United States. The President tries to make life better for the country's citizens. The President takes this responsibility seriously.

The President of the United States lives and works in the White House. People come to the White House daily to meet with the President. Some of these people make the laws in the United States. Some are from other countries. They talk about politics and how they can help Americans and others around the world.

The President tries to make decisions that keep people safe. The President also travels to give speeches about our country and to talk to people all over the country.

Talk About It What does the President do? Complete the sentences below.

The President meets with _____.

The President tries to _____.

Your Turn What do you think is the hardest part of the President's job? Why?

Defining Telling the meaning of a word is called defining it. We give information about the word. We tell what something is. The example below defines the job of the President of the United States. It tells what the job is.

Example:
> The job of the President of the United States is to lead the government.

The chart below shows other examples of defining.

Word	Defining Sentence
United States	The United States is a country.
speech	A speech is a talk given to many people.
responsibility	A responsibility is something a person has to do.

Talk About It Think about the responsibilities of your teacher. Say a sentence that defines one of his or her responsibilities.

Use the sentence frame below to help you.

> One responsibility of my teacher is _____ .

Your Turn Complete each sentence below. Define the word in bold text.

A **job** is _____ .

A **president** is _____ .

A **responsibility** I have is _____ .

Main Idea and Details The **main idea** of a paragraph is what the paragraph is mostly about. **Details** are smaller pieces of information that tell more about the main idea.

Circle the main idea of this paragraph. Underline the details that give more information about the main idea.

The President is very busy. He meets with leaders. He talks with citizens. He travels around the world.

. . . .

Talk About It What are the President's responsibilities?

Underline the details that define the responsibilities of the President.

The President of the United States has many responsibilities. One responsibility is to head the government. A second responsibility is to meet with leaders around the world. A third responsibility is to help citizens with their concerns.

. . . .

Your Turn Read the first paragraph of the passage on page 81.

What is the main idea of the paragraph? Write it below.

_____

_____

Plural Possessive Nouns A **plural possessive noun** shows that something belongs to two or more people or things. You can form a plural possessive noun by adding an apostrophe after the *-s* of a plural noun. The plural possessive nouns are circled in the sentences below.

Plural Noun	Plural Possessive Noun	Sentence	Explanation
girls	girls'	The President read the (girls') letters.	The letters belong to the girls.
leaders	leaders'	The President discussed the (leaders') concerns.	The concerns belong to the leaders.
students	students'	The (students') responsibility is to learn.	The responsibility belongs to the students.

Talk About It Read the sentences and circle the plural possessive nouns. Explain who or what has something.

> The boys' soccer team spoke to the President.
>
> The citizens' concerns are very important.
>
> The President will meet with the countries' leaders.

Your Turn Write three sentences, using one of the following plural possessive nouns.

(citizens') _____

(jobs') _____

(teachers') _____

Think, Talk, and Write

U.S. Government Think about the job of the President of the United States. Talk with a partner about how the President helps the country.

How does the President help schools?

How does the President help workers?

Talk About It Review the vocabulary on page 80. Work with a partner to tell about each word. Which words will you use to write about the President of the United States?

Produce Language Write a report about one job of the President. First complete the chart. Then write 4 to 5 sentences in your Weekly Concept Journal.

The job of the President that I will write about: _____

_____

Why it is important: _____

_____

Vocabulary words I can use: _____

_____

Hear it!
See it!
Do it!

- Big Question Video
- Concept Talk Video
- Envision It! Animation
- Grammar Jammer

Patterns in Nature

What are some patterns in nature?

The Seasons
What changes in nature take place in the fall?

Animal Migration
What patterns in nature guide the lives of animals?

Day and Night
How have people explained the pattern of day and night?

Storms
How do weather patterns affect our lives?

Changes in Nature
What causes changes in nature?

Patterns in Nature

Vocabulary

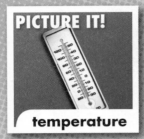

frost

temperature

autumn
climates
fascinated
seasons

What changes in nature take place in the fall?

There are four seasons. They are winter, summer, spring, and fall. Each season brings many changes in nature. In cooler climates, leaves change colors in the fall.

Read the passage together.
Then circle the vocabulary words.

The Fall Season

Fall, or ⸰autumn⸰, is one of the four ⸰seasons⸰. It is the season between summer and winter. The days grow shorter in fall because our part of Earth gets less light from the sun. The temperature changes and the weather becomes cooler. Many animals begin to travel to warmer climates where food is easier to find.

In many places, trees change in the fall. The green leaves turn red, yellow, and orange. People have always been fascinated by the beauty of fall colors. Many travel each fall to our national parks and forests to see the different colors. The leaves soon drop off the trees and the winter frost begins.

Talk About It What changes happen in the fall? Complete the sentences below.

In autumn, _____ .

Autumn can cause leaves to _____ .

Many people enjoy _____ in the fall.

Your Turn Think about autumn where you live. What do you like to do in autumn? Tell a partner about your autumn experiences.

Cause-and-Effect Relationship We often use words to tell why things happen. One of these words is *if*.

Examples: **If** it rains, I will need an umbrella.
If I had boots, I would have dry feet.
I always go indoors **if** I see lightning.
If it is sunny tomorrow,
we will play outside.

Talk About It Think about what you might do if it is cold outside. Use the sentence frame below as you discuss this with a partner.

If it is cold outside, _____ .

Your Turn Write a sentence about what you would do if it is cold outside.

_____

_____

_____

Cause and Effect A **cause** is why something happens. An **effect** is what happens.

Some words, such as *if* and *because,* show us that a sentence is telling about cause and effect.

> If the weather is very cold, lakes will freeze in winter.

Underline the cause and circle the effect in the example above.

Talk About It Look at the sentences below. With a partner, decide what is the cause and what is the effect in each sentence.

> I wear gloves in winter because it is cold.
>
> If there is ice on the road, drivers should slow down.
>
> When the weather becomes cold, many animals go somewhere warmer.

Your Turn Look back at the passage on page 89. Write one sentence that shows a cause and effect. Underline the cause and circle the effect in the sentence you write.

_____

_____

_____

Action and Linking Verbs Verbs can show actions, or things you do, such as *run* or *eat.* These are **action verbs.** Verbs can also connect the subject with other words that describe it. These are **linking verbs.**

Action Verbs	Linking Verbs
Flowers (grow) in the spring.	The flowers (are) pink.
I (swim) in the summer.	Swimming (is) fun.
Leaves (drop) from some trees in November.	The leaves (are) orange and yellow.
I (wear) gloves on my hands in winter.	My hands (are) warm in my gloves.

Talk About It Circle the verbs in the following sentences. Are they action verbs or linking verbs? Discuss with a partner how you know.

The clouds are white and fluffy.

Two children skated on the ice.

Your Turn Fill in the blanks with the correct verb in parentheses.

People _____ boots to protect their feet from snow. (wear, is)

The sun _____ hot in July. (runs, is)

Apples _____ ready to eat in summer and fall. (are, drop)

Think, Talk, and Write

The Seasons Think about the changes that take place during fall.
Talk with a partner about the things that happen when the seasons change.

How will fall change
an apple orchard?

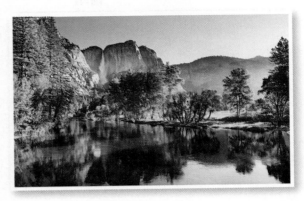

How will fall change
Yosemite Park?

Talk About It Review the vocabulary on page 88. Work with a
partner to tell about each word. Which words will you use to
write about your favorite season?

Produce Language Write about a season and tell about its
changes. First complete the chart. Then write 4 to 5 sentences
in your Weekly Concept Journal.

My season: _____

_____

What happens: _____

_____

Why it is special: _____

_____

Vocabulary words I can use: _____

_____

Vocabulary

formation

tropical

biologists

guide

migrate

navigate

pattern

What patterns in nature guide the lives of animals?

Nature has many patterns. There are patterns we can see, such as the stripes on a zebra. Seasons also occur in patterns. When seasons change, many plants and animals change.

Read the passage together.
Then circle the vocabulary words.

Bird Migration

Many birds migrate to warmer climates in the fall. Some birds fly to tropical areas. The weather is warm there, and food is easier to find. Some birds migrate in a formation, or pattern of flying.

Birds often travel thousands of miles when they migrate. They do not have maps or directions. Yet they are able to navigate to the correct place every year.

Biologists don't know exactly how birds navigate. Some biologists think birds use the sun, the stars, and the landscape to guide them. Others believe that Earth's magnetic field helps the birds know where to go. Bird migration is a pattern that happens year after year.

Talk About It Why do birds migrate?
Complete the sentences below with a partner.

> Birds migrate because _____.
>
> Biologists think birds use _____ to help them know where to go.

Your Turn What patterns are part of bird migration? Think of a sentence that tells one or two patterns in bird migration. Tell a partner.

Expressing and Supporting Opinions We sometimes talk or write about our feelings about something. We use words such as *I believe* or *I think*. These statements are opinions. However, we can use reasons to support opinions. We use the word *because* to explain our opinions.

Examples:

I think that bears are interesting animals **because** they store enough fat in their bodies to sleep all winter!

I believe that flowers are pretty **because** they come in many different colors.

Talk About It Say an opinion about this picture. Give at least two reasons to support your opinion. Use the sentence frame below to help you.

> I believe _____ because _____ and _____ .

Your Turn Write a sentence that states your opinion about this picture.

_____

_____

_____

FORM & FUNCTION

Fact and Opinion A statement that can be proven true is called a **fact.** A statement that is one person's belief about something is called an **opinion.** When people state an opinion, they sometimes use the phrase *I think* or *I believe.*

Examples:

> **Fact:** Some birds migrate before it gets cold where they live.
>
> **Opinion:** I think it would be fun to spend winter in a warm place, because I could go swimming all year.

You cannot prove that the opinion above is true, but an opinion can include reasons, or support.

- -

Talk About It Which statements are facts and which statements are opinions?

Decide with a partner why each statement is a fact or an opinion.

> The best part of summer is going swimming.
>
> Animals migrate because they need to be in warmer weather.
>
> I believe California is a fun place to be in the winter.

- -

Your Turn Look back at the passage on page 95 and write two facts. Then write an opinion about one of the facts. Be sure to include reasons to support your opinion.

_____

_____

Main Verbs and Helping Verbs Sometimes a verb is made up of more than one word. The more important word in the verb is the **main verb.** The word or words with it are called **helping verbs.**

The helping verbs are circled in the examples below.

Common Helping Verbs	Example
am, is, are, was, were	We (are) watching the birds migrate.
have, has, had	We (have) watched the birds migrate in the past.
do, does, did	Birds (do) migrate every year.
will, can, shall	Biologists (can) track bird migration on a map.
may, might, must	We (may) travel this winter too.
could, would, should	We (could) take a trip to a tropical place.

Talk About It Read the sentences. Circle the main verb in each sentence. Underline the helping verb.

Some butterflies will migrate each year.

People can enjoy the beauty of butterflies.

Your Turn Finish the sentence with a main verb and a helping verb. Then write a sentence of your own. Use a main verb and a helping verb.

Birds _____ _____ to a tropical climate in the fall.

_____

_____

Think, Talk, and Write

Animal Migration Think about how the birds migrate thousands of miles to live where there is more food and water. Talk with a partner about other animals that have patterns of migration.

Why do whales migrate?

Why do fish migrate?

Talk About It Review the vocabulary on page 94. Work with a partner to tell about each word. Which words will you use to write about animal migration patterns?

Produce Language Find information about an animal or animal group and tell how and why it migrates. You can also use the passage on page 95 to help. Then complete the chart. Then write 4 to 5 sentences in your Weekly Concept Journal.

My animal: _____

_____

Where my animal migrates: _____

_____

Why my animal migrates: _____

_____

Vocabulary words I can use: _____

_____

Vocabulary

brilliant

Inuit

delights
gleams
mystery
myth

How have people explained the pattern of day and night?

People have always thought about the pattern of day and night. Today, scientists can explain this pattern. Long ago, people told stories to explain this mystery.

Read the passage together.
Then circle the vocabulary words.

Annigan and Malina

The Inuit people tell many stories. They often tell this myth about the mystery of day and night.

Annigan, the moon god, delights in chasing his sister, Malina. Malina is the goddess of the sun. As Annigan chases her, he forgets to eat and gets thin. When he realizes he is hungry, he begins to eat. This causes him to get large and round. Then he returns to chase Malina. This is why the moon sometimes looks thin, sometimes goes away, and sometimes looks full.

Malina will not share the sky with Annigan. So, the sun shares her brilliant light during the day, while the moon gleams at night.

. . . .

Talk About It How does the story of Annigan and Malina explain day and night? Complete the sentences below.

Annigan is _____ .

Malina is _____ .

The moon _____ .

. . . .

Your Turn Why did the Inuit people tell the myth about Annigan and Malina? Write a sentence.

_____

_____

Generalizing Words that express ideas and feelings, such as *sadness* and *beauty*, are abstract nouns. An abstract noun names something you cannot touch or see. These words are often used when we generalize, or make a statement about a group of people or things.

Examples:
People have **curiosity** about why the moon appears to change shape.

People feel **joy** when they see the sun rise.

I have a lot of **love** for my family.

Talk About It With a partner, circle the abstract nouns in the sentences below that express ideas and feelings.

The glow of the light gave me comfort.

My fear grew as the sun went down.

Some people think a full moon brings bad luck.

Your Turn Use the following abstract nouns that express ideas or feelings to fill in the blanks: *joy, sympathy, talent.*

I feel a lot of _____ for my friend because her dog died.

My friend, who plays the piano, has a lot of _____.

When I looked up at the moon, I felt _____.

Generalize Sometimes when we read, we can **generalize,** or make a statement about a group of people or things together. Clue words, such as *most, all, always,* and *never,* often show generalizations. Sometimes generalizations use abstract nouns that express ideas or feelings.

There are many stories that tell why there is day and night. These stories come from countries around the world. Many of the stories are very old.

Generalization: People have **always** looked for reasons to explain why we have day and night.

Talk About It With a partner, circle the clue word that helps you know each sentence is a generalization.

Most people like to look at the moon.

All people like to look through a telescope.

Fourth graders always like to play.

Your Turn Reread the passage on page 101. Write a generalization about day and night. Underline the clue word.

_____

_____

_____

Subject-Verb Agreement Subjects and verbs must go together. This is called **subject-verb agreement.** In the chart below, subjects are circled and verbs are underlined.

Singular	Plural
The boy looks at the moon.	The boys look at the moon.
My brother sleeps during the day.	My brothers sleep during the day.
The girl is outside.	The girls are outside.

Talk About It Read the sentences below. Choose the correct verb in parentheses to fill in the blank.

The clouds _____ in front of the moon. (is, are)

The sun _____ bright today. (were, was)

Your Turn Finish these sentences with the correct word or words in parentheses.

_____ are shining in the night sky. (A star, Stars)

The flowers _____ enough sunlight to grow. (need, needs)

The _____ looks big. (clouds, cloud)

Think, Talk, and Write

Day and Night Think about how the Inuit people explained the pattern of day and night. What other things do people wonder about day and night?

Why does the sun shine so bright?

Why does the moon's shape seem to change?

. . . .

Talk About It Review the vocabulary on page 100. Work with a partner to tell about each word. Which words will you use to write a story about day and night?

. . . .

Produce Language Write your own myth that tells about the pattern of day and night. First complete the chart. Then write 4 to 5 sentences in your Weekly Concept Journal.

My characters: _____

_____

What happens: _____

_____

My reason for day and night: _____

_____

Vocabulary words I can use: _____

_____

Vocabulary

destruction

funnel

radar

forecasts
rotates
unstable
violent

How do weather patterns affect our lives?

Weather affects our lives in many ways. Rain, snow, and temperatures affect what we do each day. Storms, such as hurricanes and tornadoes, seriously affect our lives.

Read the passage together.
Then circle the vocabulary words.

Tornadoes

Tornadoes are one of nature's most (violent) storms. The United States has about 800 tornadoes each year. These storms cause about 80 deaths and 1,500 injuries each year. Tornadoes also cause millions of dollars in (destruction).

A tornado is a cloud of turning air that is shaped like a funnel. Warm and cold air meet, which makes the air unstable. The air lifts and rotates, creating a tornado.

A tornado can travel many miles and can have winds that move more than 250 miles per hour.

Scientists use radar to track tornadoes so they can give forecasts to people. These forecasts can help warn people to get to a safe place.

· ·

Talk About It What makes a tornado dangerous? Complete the sentences below.

Tornadoes are storms that can _____.

When warm air and cold air meet, _____.

Radar helps scientists _____.

· ·

Your Turn Think about severe weather you know about or have heard about. Describe the severe weather to a partner.

Describing We use words to describe things. Sometimes we use phrases, or groups of words that work together, to describe something. We can use these words that answer the question *where?* to describe where something is.

Example:

> The storm is **in California.**
>
> Our storm shelter is **in the basement.**

Circle the words that answer the question *where?* in the sentences below.

On top of, above	We saw dark clouds above our house.
In front of	The storm was in front of us.
Beside, next to	A tornado was seen in the town next to us.
Beneath, under, below	The safest place to be during a tornado is in the basement beneath our house.

· ·

Talk About It Look at the pictures and fill in the blanks with location words.

The funnel cloud is
_____ the sky.

The rain is falling
_____ the ground.

· ·

Your Turn Imagine you are in the city during the storm pictured above. Write a sentence to describe where you would be. Use words that answer the question *where?*

_____

Graphic Sources Words give information.
Graphic sources also give information. A photograph is an example of a graphic source. A chart is also a graphic source.

A graphic source sometimes has words that describe things in the graphic source. These words are called labels.

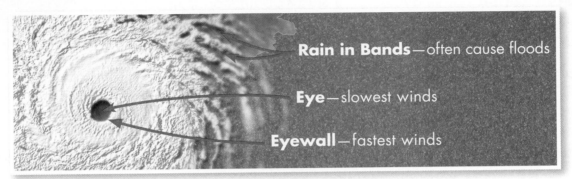

Rain in Bands—often cause floods

Eye—slowest winds

Eyewall—fastest winds

Talk About It Look at the graphic source about hurricanes. What information does the graphic source give you about hurricanes?

Complete the sentences below with a partner.

The slowest winds in a hurricane are _____ .

The _____ winds in a hurricane are in the eyewall.

The heaviest rain in a hurricane is _____ .

Your Turn Look at the graphic source of the hurricane. Write two sentences to describe the storm. Use the sentences above as a model.

_____

_____

_____

_____

Past, Present, and Future Tenses Actions happen in the **present, past,** or **future.** Verbs have different forms for different tenses. Sometimes the future tense needs a helping verb.

	Verb	Sentence
Present Tense	study	I study about storms in school.
Past Tense	studied	I studied about hurricanes yesterday.
Future Tense	will study	I will study about tornadoes tomorrow.

Talk About It Read the sentences below with a partner.

Circle the verbs and tell the tense.

The wind blew during the storm.

Rain from hurricanes will cause floods.

Your Turn Finish each sentence with *rains, rained,* or *will rain.*

The forecast says it _____ tomorrow.

Last year it _____ on my birthday.

It _____ during a storm.

Think, Talk, and Write

Storms Think about tornadoes and how they can cause so much destruction to buildings and people. Talk with a partner about other kinds of storms that affect our lives.

How can a drought affect our lives?

How can a snowstorm affect our lives?

Talk About It Review the vocabulary on page 106. Work with a partner to tell about each word. Which words will you use to write about how a weather pattern can affect your life?

Produce Language Write about a storm and how it would cause your life to change. First complete the chart. Then write 4 to 5 sentences in your Weekly Concept Journal.

The storm: _____

_____

The destruction: _____

_____

How it would affect my life: _____

_____

Vocabulary words I can use: _____

_____

Vocabulary

cowboy

lasso

challenge

harness

refused

sea level

untamed

What causes changes in nature?

Nature is always changing. For example, rivers can make valleys. Sometimes scientists can explain these changes. Yet for hundreds of years, people have also made up stories to explain these changes. There are even cowboy stories that explain changes in nature!

Read the passage together.
Then circle the vocabulary words.

Cowboy Pecos Bill

Pecos Bill was the greatest cowboy in history! He could ride anything, even the most untamed horse.

One day, Pecos Bill was riding his horse in Kansas. The sky became dark. Out of nowhere, a tornado appeared! Pecos Bill loved a challenge. So, he threw his lasso around that tornado. He used the rope as a harness and rode the tornado like a horse! That tornado twisted and turned, but Bill refused to let go. He rode that tornado all the way to California.

Bill finally fell off. He hit the ground with such force that it sank below sea level! People now call that place Death Valley. It is one of the lowest places on Earth.

- -

Talk About It How was Pecos Bill a great cowboy? Complete the sentences below.

Pecos Bill was a great cowboy because _____.

Bill _____ the tornado.

When Bill fell off the tornado, _____.

- -

Your Turn Write two sentences about what you would do if a tornado appeared. Use at least one vocabulary word.

Asking Questions When we read, sometimes we ask ourselves questions to get more information. We use *who, what, where, when, why,* and *how* when we ask questions. For example, you might ask questions about the sentence below.

Sentence: The cowboy grabbed his lasso.

Question: **Why** did he grab the lasso?

Question: **What** do cowboys do with lassos?

. . . .

Talk About It Read the following sentence and tell your partner a question you would ask yourself.

A tornado came through the town where the girl was living.

. . . .

Your Turn Read the following sentence and write two questions you might ask yourself.

Pecos Bill loved being a cowboy.

_____

_____

_____

_____

Generalize When we read, we often **generalize.** This means that we make a general statement about something that we don't have a lot of information on. Words such as *most, all, always,* and *never* are used to make generalizations. We often ask questions before we generalize.

In the Old West, cowboys took care of the cattle and horses. The work of cowboys was very important in the Old West. Many stories tell about life in the Old West.

Question: What do we know about cowboys in stories about the Old West?

Generalization: Cowboys are probably in **many** stories about the Old West.

Talk About It Read the following and make a generalization.

> Cowboys are good at taking care of cattle. They are also good at taking care of horses.

Your Turn Read the following sentences and write a generalization.

> The tornado destroyed 500 homes. It hurt many people too.

_____

_____

115

Irregular Verbs To form the past tense of regular verbs in English, we add *-ed.* Some verbs do not follow this rule. These are called **irregular verbs.** Examples of common irregular verbs are circled in the chart below.

Present Tense	Past Tense
Cowboys catch runaway horses.	Cowboys caught runaway horses.
Cowboys ride their horses.	Cowboys rode their horses.
Cowboys sleep on the ground.	Cowboys slept on the ground.
Cowboys teach each other to use lassos.	Cowboys taught each other to use lassos.

Talk About It Read the sentences and circle the verbs.

Cowboys usually wore boots.

An untamed horse threw the cowboy onto the ground.

Your Turn Finish the sentences with the correct form of the verb in parentheses.

My teacher _____ us about Pecos Bill last week.
(teaches, taught)

People in the Old West _____ horses and trains.
(ride, rode)

Changes in Nature Think about the story of Pecos Bill and how he created Death Valley when he fell off the tornado. Talk with a partner about other ways that changes in nature can be explained with a funny story.

What caused this crater?

What caused this cave?

Talk About It Review the vocabulary on page 112. Work with a partner to tell about each word. Which words will you use to write a story about a change in nature?

Produce Language Write a funny story that explains how a change happened in nature. You may want to explain one of the pictures above. First complete the chart. Then write 4 to 5 sentences in your Weekly Concept Journal.

My change in nature: _____

_____

Where the change takes place: _____

_____

The characters in the story: _____

_____

Vocabulary words I can use: _____

_____

Get Online!

Hear it!
See it!
Do it!

- Big Question Video
- Concept Talk Video
- Envision It! Animation
- Grammar Jammer

Puzzles and Mysteries

 Is there an explanation for everything?

Perception
Can you always believe what you see?

Animal Behavior
Why do animals behave the way they do?

Secret Codes
Why are secret codes necessary?

Communication
How can knowing another language create understanding?

Inquiry
How can attention to detail help solve a problem?

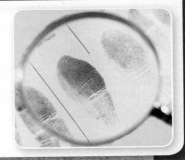

Puzzles and Mysteries

audience

magician

assistant
distract
escape
illusion
performing

Can you always believe what you see?

We cannot always believe what we see. Sometimes our eyes are tricked. A person may do a magic trick that seems unbelievable. Great magicians, such as Houdini, fooled many people with their tricks.

Vocabulary in Context

Read the passage together.
Then circle the vocabulary words.

The Great Houdini

Harry Houdini was a (magician). He lived about 100 years ago. He was famous because he could (escape) from almost anything. But this was an illusion. Houdini only made it look like he could escape from almost anything. He was performing magic tricks.

In one trick, Houdini escaped from a rope. First an assistant would tie a long rope around him. The assistant would knot the rope tightly. Then Houdini would escape from the rope while an audience watched him. Houdini talked to his audience to distract them. They wouldn't notice him cut the rope. That was the secret of his escape.

. . . .

Talk About It Why was Houdini famous?
Complete the sentences below.

Houdini could escape _____ .

Houdini was good at _____ .

Houdini tricked audiences by _____ .

. . . .

Your Turn This magician is pulling a rabbit out of a hat. The hat was empty before. Write a sentence about why this is hard to believe.

_____

_____

Comparing and Contrasting We use words to show how things are alike and different. Words such as *both* and *like* are used to tell how things are alike. Words such as *but* and *unlike* are used to tell how things are different.

Word	Sentence	What Is Alike or Different?
both	Houdini could escape from **both** rope and handcuffs.	The rope and handcuffs are **alike.**
like	Gina, **like** her friends, could not believe what she saw.	Gina and her friends are **alike.**
but	Some magicians tell their secrets, **but** other magicians do not.	Some magicians are **different** from other magicians.
unlike	**Unlike** many magicians, Houdini became famous.	Many magicians are **different** from Houdini.

Talk About It Say a sentence that tells how these two rabbits are alike. Use *both* or *like* in your sentence.

Your Turn Write a sentence that tells how these rabbits are different. Use *but* or *unlike* in your sentence.

_____

_____

Comprehension Support

Compare and Contrast Sometimes we read passages or stories that compare and contrast. When we **compare,** we show how things are alike. When we **contrast,** we show how things are different. Clue words, such as *and, both, like, but,* and *unlike,* may tell when things are being compared or contrasted.

Talk About It Read each sentence below. Say whether it compares or contrasts.

Find the compare and contrast clue words with your partner.

> Jorge and Ellie both think magic shows are fun. Like Jorge, Ellie does not always believe the magic is real. Unlike Jorge, Ellie wants to know the secrets of the magicians.

Your Turn Compare the magician on the right with the two young magicians pictured above.

Write a sentence that compares the magicians. Use *and* or *like* in your comparison.

_____

_____

_____

_____

Singular and Plural Pronouns A pronoun is a word that is used instead of the name of a person, place, or thing. A **singular pronoun** stands for one person, place, or thing. A **plural pronoun** stands for more than one person, place, or thing. Singular and plural pronouns are listed below.

Singular Pronouns	→	Plural Pronouns
I	→	we
you	→	you
he	→	they
she	→	they
it	→	they

Talk About It Read the sentences with a partner. Circle the pronouns. Tell if they are singular or plural pronouns.

I went to the magic show with Amy. We liked seeing the magician's tricks. He escaped from a locked box without help. You would have been amazed! It was a great show.

Your Turn Write a sentence about the person in the picture. Start your sentence with a pronoun.

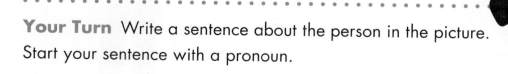

_____

_____

Think, Talk, and Write

Perception Think about how Harry Houdini created illusions. Talk with a partner about a time when you could not believe what you saw.

How can an image create an illusion?

How can art create an illusion?

Talk About It Review the vocabulary on page 120. Work with a partner to tell about each word. Which words will you use to write about a time when you could not believe your eyes?

Produce Language Write a story about a time when you could not believe what you saw. First complete the chart. Then write 4 to 5 sentences in your Weekly Concept Journal.

What I thought I saw: _____

_____

What I really saw: _____

_____

How it made me feel: _____

_____

Vocabulary words I can use: _____

_____

Vocabulary

communicate

migration

aquatic
behave
enchanted
mates
surface

Why do animals behave the way they do?

Animals behave, or act, in different ways. Some animals, like whales, communicate with each other with noises or songs. Other animals do not seem to communicate. We do not always know why animals behave the way they do.

Vocabulary in Context

Read the passage together.
Then circle the vocabulary words.

Whale Songs

Whales sing deep below the water's surface. But the singing of whales is not like our singing. Whales make high squeaks, low rumbles, and other sounds.

Whale songs may have patterns. Whales often sing the same patterns again and again. Whales that live near one another often know the same patterns. What do the patterns mean?

Whales may sing to find mates. Whales may use singing to communicate with one another during migration. Scientists are not sure why whales behave this way. Scientists are enchanted with the songs of these aquatic animals. But they still have a lot to learn.

• •

Talk About It What do scientists know about whale singing? Complete the sentences below.

Whales may sing to _____ .

The patterns of whale songs are _____ .

• •

Your Turn Look at the picture of the dog. Write a sentence about how the dog is behaving and why you think that.

_____

_____

Language Workshop

Describing We use adjectives to describe people, places, and things. Adjectives help us tell about things. Adjectives tell about size, color, sound, and many other things.

Circle the adjectives in the sentences in the chart.

Adjective	What the Adjective Describes	Sentences
aquatic	dolphins	Dolphins are aquatic.
barking	dogs	The barking dogs protect the house.
two, gray	whales	The two gray whales sing songs.

- -

Talk About It Say a sentence that describes the giraffe in the picture. Use two adjectives in your sentence.

- -

Your Turn Write a sentence that describes the elephant in the picture. Use at least two adjectives in your sentence. Circle the adjectives you use.

_____

_____

Categorize and Classify We **categorize,** or **classify,** when we put things that are alike into groups. Classifying and categorizing help us understand what we read.

mouse	snake	spider
frog	dog	lion

You could classify the animals above into two groups: animals with tails and animals without tails.

Animals with Tails	Animals without Tails
mouse, dog, lion	snake, spider, frog

Talk About It Read the sentences below. How can you classify all of the animals?

Think of two different groups in which all of these animals can fit.

> A goldfish lives in a fishbowl. Sharks live in the ocean. Whales also live in the ocean.

Your Turn Look at the pictures. How are these three things alike?

Write a sentence that tells how you could classify these things.

_____

_____

Grammar

Subject and Object Pronouns Pronouns are words that take the place of nouns. **Subject pronouns** tell who or what is doing something. **Object pronouns** come after the verb or after the preposition.

Subject Pronouns	Object Pronouns
I like to learn about whales.	Aquatic animals interest me.
You should tell the dog to sit.	The dog will sit for you.
He pointed at the birds.	The birds flew above him.
She saw a snake.	The snake was behind her.
It flew into the sky.	I saw it fly away.
We did not see any fish.	The fish did not swim near us.
They live in the water.	Scientists study them.

Talk About It Complete each sentence with one of the pronouns.

(He, Him) _____ knows a lot about animals.

Animals behave in ways that surprise _____. (we, us)

Your Turn Write two sentences. Use the pronouns listed below.

(them) _____

(you) _____

Think, Talk, and Write

Animal Behavior Think about how the whales use sounds to communicate with each other. Talk with a partner about why animals behave the way they do.

Why do dogs bark?

Why do birds sing?

Talk About It Review the vocabulary on page 126. Work with a partner to tell about each word. Which words will you use to write about how animals use patterns to communicate?

Produce Language Write about an animal and how it communicates. First complete the chart. Then write 4 to 5 sentences in your Weekly Concept Journal.

My animal: _____

_____

How my animal communicates: _____

_____

Why my animal behaves this way: _____

_____

Vocabulary words I can use: _____

_____

Vocabulary

PICTURE IT!

route

PICTURE IT!

station

abolitionists
enslaved
exhausting
messages
protected

Why are secret codes necessary?

People have used secret codes for many years. The codes can keep enemies from learning about secret plans. In this way, secret codes can protect people and information.

Read the passage together.
Then circle the vocabulary words.

The Underground Railroad Code

The Underground Railroad was a secret route that helped enslaved Africans travel from the South to the North. Until the 1860s, many Africans were enslaved in the South. They were forced to work and were not paid. When enslaved people traveled to the North, they could be protected. They were free.

Abolitionists used codes to help enslaved Africans on their exhausting trip. Many code words came from real railroads. A safe house on the route was called a "station," like a railroad station.

Enslaved people sent messages to one another in songs. For example, they might sing a song about following the North Star. The song's words would tell which direction to go to escape.

Talk About It How were codes a part of the Underground Railroad? Complete the sentences below with a partner.

Abolitionists used codes to _____.

Songs could be codes because _____.

Your Turn Say a sentence about why secret codes were important for enslaved Africans. Tell a partner.

Secret codes helped enslaved Africans because _____.

133

Sequencing Events happen in a certain order. Words that answer the question *when?*, such as *already, finally,* and *eventually,* can help us tell the order in which things happen.

Circle the clue word in each sentence below.

When?	Sentence
already	We already sent the message using a secret code.
finally	The enslaved people finally became free.
eventually	Eventually, the enslaved people reached the next station.

Talk About It Say a sentence about the Underground Railroad. Use words that answer the question *when?* in your sentence.

Finally, _____ .

Your Turn Write a sentence that uses a word from the box above that answers the question *when?*

_____

_____

Sequence When we read a story, the events are usually told in the order in which they happen. This order is called the **sequence.** Words such as *already, finally, eventually,* and *still* help to show sequence.

Circle the first event that happened.
Underline the last event that happened.

Kim found a pencil and a piece of paper. She wrote a message in code. Then she sent it to her friend Ben. Ben eventually figured out what the message said. It said: "Meet me at the park!"

· ·

Talk About It What is the sequence of the events below?

Number the events in the order in which they happened.

_____ The enslaved Africans were finally free.

_____ Some enslaved Africans wanted to escape and travel to the North.

_____ The enslaved Africans traveled along the Underground Railroad.

· ·

Your Turn Read the sentences above.

Write the sentences in order.

_____

_____

_____

_____

Grammar

Pronouns and Antecedents **Pronouns** are words that take the place of nouns. **Antecedents** are the nouns that the pronouns replace.

Sentence with Antecedent	Sentence with Pronoun
The woman knows a secret code.	**She** knows a secret code.
Jay and Jack are abolitionists.	**They** are abolitionists.
Enslaved Africans followed the **Underground Railroad** to the North.	Enslaved Africans followed **it** to the North.

Talk About It Read the sentences and circle the pronouns. Underline their antecedents.

Enslaved Africans used code words. The code words helped them communicate.

Stu is writing a secret code. Will he finish it today?

Your Turn Rewrite each sentence. Use a pronoun to replace the boldface words.

The girl told her friend a secret.

_____

The book showed many secret codes.

_____

Think, Talk, and Write

Secret Codes Think about how the abolitionists and enslaved people used secret codes on the Underground Railroad. Talk with a partner about when you might use a secret code.

Do you need a code to tell a secret?

Do soldiers need a secret code?

Talk About It Review the vocabulary on page 132. Work with a partner to tell about each word. Which words will you use to write about a secret code?

Produce Language Write a story about how a secret code helps people. First complete the chart. Then write 4 to 5 sentences in your Weekly Concept Journal.

The people who need help: _____

_____

The secret code: _____

_____

What happens: _____

_____

How to read the secret code: _____

_____

Vocabulary words I can use: _____

_____

Communication

Vocabulary

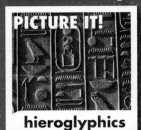
hieroglyphics

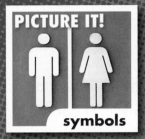
symbols

ancient
official
scholars
traditional
translate

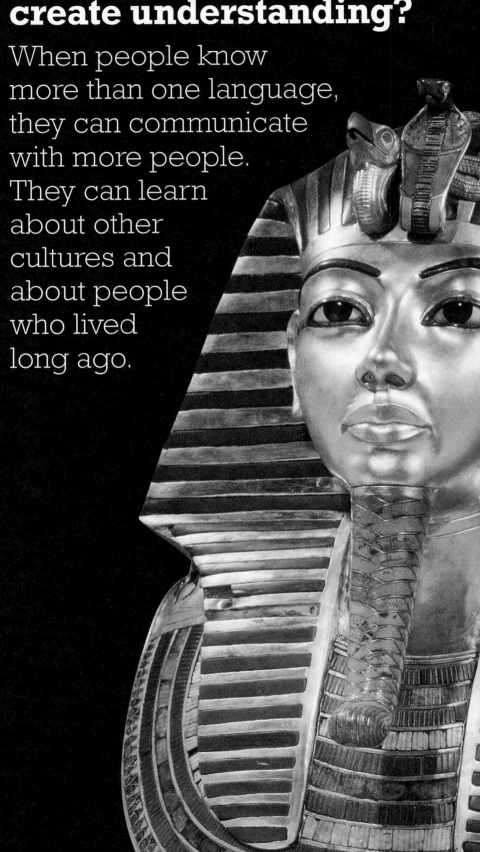

How can knowing another language create understanding?

When people know more than one language, they can communicate with more people. They can learn about other cultures and about people who lived long ago.

Read the passage together.
Then circle the vocabulary words.

KING TUT

King Tutankhamen, or King Tut, was a ruler of ancient Egypt. King Tut was around ten years old when he became king, and he ruled for nine years. King Tut changed the official religion of ancient Egypt. He brought back traditional arts that his father had not allowed.

King Tut lived thousands of years ago. But scholars are still learning new things about him. These scholars know about hieroglyphics. This is the written language of ancient Egypt. Scholars translate the pictures and symbols. This helps them learn about King Tut and understand the culture of ancient Egypt.

· ·

Talk About It What have scholars learned about King Tut and ancient Egypt? Complete the sentences below.

King Tut was _____ .

King Tut changed ancient Egypt by _____ .

The written language of ancient Egypt _____ .

· ·

Your Turn What can ancient languages help us understand? Share your ideas with a partner. Use the selection above to help you.

Language Workshop FORM & FUNCTION

Retelling We use the past tense of verbs when we are telling about things that happened in the past. Many past tense verbs end in *-ed*, but others do not.

Read the sentences in the chart. The verbs are circled.

Present Tense (Happening Now)	Past Tense (Already Happened)
She (writes) with pictures and symbols.	She (wrote) with pictures and symbols.
The scholars (study) hieroglyphics.	The scholars (studied) hieroglyphics.
Brian (learns) the Spanish language.	Brian (learned) the Spanish language.
They (talk) in English.	They (talked) in English.

Talk About It Say a sentence about something that happened while you were learning English. Use a past tense verb in your sentence.

Your Turn Write a sentence about something that happened yesterday. Use a past tense verb in your sentence.

_____

_____

Graphic Sources Charts and pictures are examples of **graphic sources.** They can make a text easier to understand. A time line is also a graphic source. A time line shows when events happened in the past. Look at the time line below. It shows some events in ancient Egypt.

Title: Ancient Egypt Time Line

3100 – 2950 B.C. Egyptians started using hieroglyphics.

2575 – 2150 B.C. Egyptians built the Great Pyramids.

1333 B.C. King Tut became ruler of Egypt.

1323 B.C. King Tut died.

Talk About It What can you learn from the time line?

With a partner, use information from the time line to complete the sentence.

_____ before King Tut became ruler of Egypt.

Your Turn Write a sentence about King Tut. Use the past tense.

_____

_____

Grammar

Possessive Pronouns Pronouns are words that take the place of nouns.
Possessive pronouns show that something belongs to someone.

The possessive pronouns are circled in the chart below.

	Singular	**Plural**
First person	(My) books are in English. The English books are (mine).	(Our) class is studying English. The English books are (ours).
Second person	Two languages are spoken in (your) home. What languages are spoken in (yours)?	I learned many things about (your) culture. This flag is (yours). 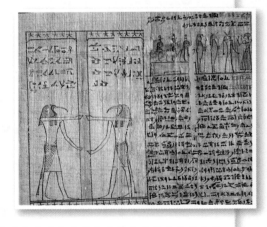
Third person	(Her) dictionary is in Spanish. The dictionary is (hers). (His) home is in Egypt. People know Paris for (its) food.	(Their) visit to the ancient pyramids was fun. Our visit was as fun as (theirs).

Talk About It Read the sentences. Circle the possessive pronouns. What noun does each possessive pronoun stand for? Tell a partner.

> King Tut ruled his country at a young age.
>
> Ancient Egyptians wrote their hieroglyphics on special paper.

Your Turn Finish these sentences. Use possessive pronouns from the chart.

The girl wrote _____ history paper about Egypt.

Ancient Egyptians were proud of _____ pyramids.

Ancient Egypt had _____ own language.

142

Think, Talk, and Write

Communication Think about how scholars learned about King Tutankhamen by translating hieroglyphics. Talk with a partner about how much we can learn about other cultures by learning other languages.

What do you think scholars learned from the Rosetta Stone?

. . . .

Talk About It Review the vocabulary on page 138. Work with a partner to tell about each word. Which words will you use to write about knowing another language?

. . . .

Produce Language Write about why it is helpful to know another language. First complete the chart. Then write 4 to 5 sentences in your Weekly Concept Journal.

My language: _____

_____

Why it is helpful to know: _____

_____

What you can learn about the culture: _____

_____

Vocabulary words I can use: _____

_____

Inquiry

Vocabulary

PICTURE IT!

detective

PICTURE IT!

diamond

attention
anticrime
crime
details
fingerprints
stumped

How can attention to detail help solve a problem?

Many problems seem too big to solve at first. But some problems can be split into smaller pieces, or details. Sometimes understanding one detail can solve the big problem.

Left Thumb

Right Hand

Vocabulary in Context

Read the passage together.
Then circle the vocabulary words.

The Missing Diamond Ring

My name is Detective Catchem. I help the police when there is a crime to solve. I am anticrime.

Today someone took Ms. Richie's diamond ring. But who? The police are stumped.

When I arrive at the crime scene, I pay attention to details. I check the jewelry box. There are no fingerprints, but the box is a little wet. I also find some short, brown hair in the box. Ms. Richie has blond hair.

I hear a scratching noise in the closet. I think I have solved the crime. I open the closet door, and there is Ms. Richie's new, brown puppy. A shiny ring hangs from his mouth.

- -

Talk About It How did details help solve the crime? Complete the sentences below with a partner.

Detective Catchem noticed that the box _____.

Detective Catchem found _____ in the closet.

- -

Your Turn Think of a time you lost something important. How did you find it? Tell a partner what you did. Use the example above to help you.

Describing An action is what someone does. When we describe action, we may tell when, where, or why the action was done. Some phrases, or groups of words, can help us describe action.

	Words That Describe Action	Examples
To Describe Why:	because… so that…	I looked in the closet because I heard a noise. (**Why** did I look in the closet? Because I heard a noise.)
To Describe When:	before… after… until… when… as soon as…	The detective came after the crime happened. (**When** did the detective come? After the crime happened.)
To Describe Where:	where… wherever…	People leave fingerprints wherever they go. (**Where** do people leave fingerprints? Wherever they go.)

Talk About It Tell about the last time you lost something. Describe when it happened. Use words that describe action.

Your Turn Finish the sentences below. Write phrases that describe why, when, or where.

I like to solve crimes _____.

Harold solved his problem _____.

Plot/Theme Plot and theme are parts of a story. **Plot** is what happens in a story. Plot has a beginning, middle, and end. **Theme** is the "big idea" of a story. Theme is what the author wants you to learn.

Look at the story on page 145. Think about what happens in the story. That is the plot. Think about what the author is trying to say about detectives and solving crimes. That is the theme.

Talk About It Read the sentences below. Which sentence tells the theme of "The Missing Diamond Ring"? Why?

Circle the theme. Talk about why you think it is the theme.

> Dogs like to eat diamonds.
>
> Looking for details can help solve a crime.
>
> All dogs hide in closets.

Your Turn What is the plot of "The Missing Diamond Ring"?

Finish the sentences with details from the story.

The police called Detective Catchem because _____.

When Detective Catchem arrived, he _____.

Detective Catchem found the diamond when _____.

Negatives and Contractions **Contractions** are two words that are made into one word. The meaning stays the same. Many contractions are made of one verb, such as *can*, and one **negative,** such as *not.* We put an apostrophe (') in a contraction to show where there are missing letters.

Example: The detective **did not** know all the details.
The detective **didn't** know all the details.

Verb + Negative	Contraction	Missing Letters
can not	can't	n, o
did not	didn't	o
was not	wasn't	o
should not	shouldn't	o

Talk About It Draw an apostrophe between the correct letters in each contraction. Talk about why you put the apostrophes where you did.

cant wasnt shouldnt didnt

Your Turn Change the bold words in each sentence to a contraction.

The detective **did not** miss important details.

_____

A puppy **was not** what Detective Catchem thought he would find.

_____

Think, Talk, and Write

Inquiry Think about how the detective found the missing ring by paying attention to details. Talk with a partner about a time when you needed to pay attention to details.

Do you use details to solve a math equation?

Do you use details to read a book?

Talk About It Review the vocabulary on page 144. Work with a partner to tell about each word. Which words will you use to write about a time when you paid attention to details to solve a problem?

Produce Language Write about a time when you paid attention to details to solve a problem. First complete the chart. Then write 4 to 5 sentences in your Weekly Concept Journal.

My problem: _____

_____

The details: _____

_____

The solution: _____

_____

Vocabulary words I can use: _____

_____

Adventures by Land, Air, and Water

THE BIG ? What makes an adventure?

Emergencies

How can we prepare for emergencies?

Ancient Civilizations

What surprises can happen on an expedition?

Heroism

What does it take to be a hero?

Adaptations to Harsh Climates

What does a person sacrifice to explore the unknown?

The Moon

What are the risks when walking on the moon?

Adventures by Land, Air, and Water

Vocabulary

PICTURE IT!

parachute

PICTURE IT!

pilot

dangerous

emergency

rescue

steer

How can we prepare for emergencies?

Emergencies can happen to anyone, especially to people with adventurous jobs. People can prepare for emergencies by learning about safety and by understanding what dangerous things might happen.

Read the passage together.
Then circle the vocabulary words.

PARACHUTE EMERGENCIES

A (pilot) has a (dangerous) job. Although airplanes are usually safe, sometimes an emergency can happen. A parachute can save a pilot's life in an air emergency. It is important that airplanes have parachutes.

However, parachutes can be difficult to steer in strong winds. Sometimes wind pushes the parachute into a tree. The pilot can get stuck in the tree or be injured.

If that happens, rescue workers, such as firefighters, rush to the scene. They carefully take the injured pilot down from the tree. Then they bring the pilot to a hospital. The pilot is well cared for there.

• •

Talk About It What happens in an air emergency? Complete the sentences below.

> Parachutes can _____.
>
> Rescue workers _____.
>
> Airplanes are _____.

• •

Your Turn Write a sentence about how a pilot can be rescued. Use the sentences above to help.

_____

_____

Defining We use words to define people and things and to tell their characteristics. A characteristic is something special about that person or thing. For example, a characteristic of water is that it is wet.

Examples: A police officer helps people in emergencies.
A firefighter is brave.

Below are some words that tell characteristics of a police officer and a firefighter.

Word	Characteristics
police officer	keeps people safe, helps people in emergencies, is brave, has a dangerous job
firefighter	fights fires, helps people in emergencies, is brave, has a dangerous job

Talk About It Say a sentence that tells about police officers. Say a sentence about firefighters. Use the characteristics above to help.

Police officers _____.

Firefighters _____.

Your Turn Write a sentence to describe a firefighter. Use the picture above.

_____

_____

Categorize and Classify When we **categorize** and **classify**, we put things into groups because they are alike in some way. For example, an apple, a strawberry, and an orange are all fruits. We can use words that describe to categorize and classify things.

Think about what rescue workers do. Circle the rescue worker pictured below.

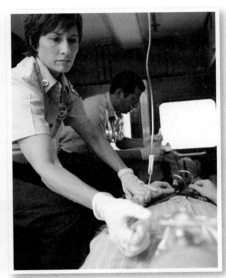

Talk About It Look at the photos above.

Talk with a partner about why the person you circled is classified as a rescue worker.

This person is a rescue worker because _____ .

Your Turn Look at the passage on page 153. A parachute is something that keeps people safe. Classify some other things that keep people safe in airplanes or cars.

_____ keep people safe in airplanes or cars.

Grammar

Adjectives and Articles A word that describes a noun or pronoun is an **adjective.** For example, *safe, happy,* and *strong* are adjectives. You can use adjectives to combine two sentences into one sentence. The words *a, an,* and *the* are called **articles.**

The adjectives and articles are circled in the chart below.

Sentence with Adjective	Sentence with Adjective	Combined Sentence
The pilot is young.	The pilot is brave.	The pilot is young and brave.
It is a new airplane.	It is a fast airplane.	It is a new, fast airplane.

Talk About It Circle the adjectives and underline the articles in the sentences below.

The flood victim was tired and wet.

The fearless firefighter put out the raging fire.

Your Turn Write two sentences containing adjectives and articles. Then combine the two sentences into one sentence.

_____

_____

_____

_____

Think, Talk, and Write

Emergencies Think about how firefighters help pilots during emergencies. Talk with a partner about other people who help after emergencies.

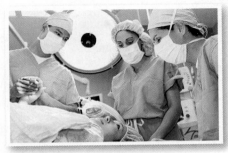

How does a doctor help in an emergency?

How can the police help in an emergency?

Talk About It Review the vocabulary on page 152. Work with a partner to tell about each word. Which words will you use to write about an emergency?

Produce Language Write about an emergency and how we prepare for it. First complete the chart. Then write 4 to 5 sentences in your Weekly Concept Journal.

My emergency: _____

_____

How we can prepare: _____

_____

Who can help: _____

_____

Vocabulary words I can use: _____

_____

PICTURE IT!

palace

PICTURE IT!

ruins

capital

destroyed

expedition

glorious

impossible

What surprises can happen on an expedition?

When an explorer goes on a trip to an unknown place, it is called an expedition. Sometimes, what is found on the trip can be amazing. However, surprises, both good and bad, can happen on any expedition.

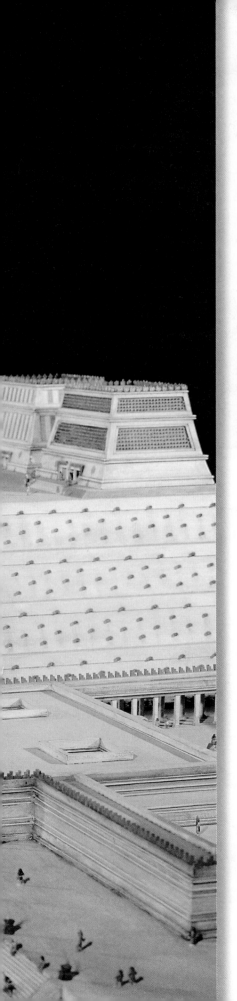

Read the passage together.
Then circle the vocabulary words.

Cortés Finds a Surprise

Over 500 years ago, Spanish explorer Hernán Cortés explored what is now Mexico. Cortés and his men rode their horses into the Aztec capital. They saw the most amazing sights.

The city was bigger than most capitals in Europe. There was a huge market filled with busy shops. People rode small boats in canals. The king lived in a huge palace with 300 rooms. The city had a zoo, a ball court, and even a pool. It was almost impossible for the men to believe their eyes.

Cortés decided to take over the city for the king of Spain. There were terrible battles between Cortés's men and the Aztecs. Much was destroyed and the glorious city lay in ruins.

• •

Talk About It What surprises happened during and as a result of Cortés's expedition? Complete the sentences below.

In the amazing Aztec capital, there were _____.

In the end, Cortés _____.

• •

Your Turn Where would you like to explore? Why? Tell a partner about it.

Comparing and Contrasting We often compare and contrast things. We tell how they are the same and different. Some words that help compare and contrast things are *but, unlike, like,* and *both*.

Example:

My city is **like** the Aztec capital, **but** my city is new. **Both** my city and the Aztec capital are big, **but** my city is bigger.

Talk About It Think about the city you know. Then look at the picture of the ancient city above. Compare and contrast the two cities.

Both cities _____ .

Unike the ancient city, my city _____ .

Your Turn Write a sentence that contrasts what the two people are wearing. Use *but* or *unlike* to make the contrast.

_____

_____

_____

Compare and Contrast When we read, we **compare** things to show how they are alike. We **contrast** things to show how they are different. Comparing and contrasting helps us understand what we read or see.

Read the diagram. Find ways the Aztecs were similar to you and how they were different.

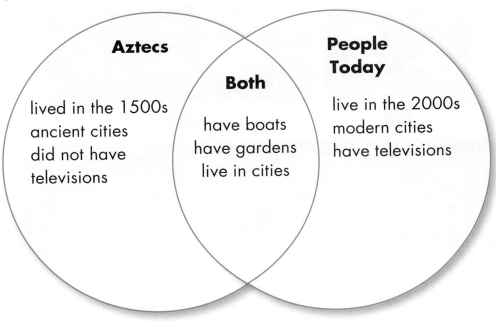

Aztecs

lived in the 1500s
ancient cities
did not have
televisions

Both

have boats
have gardens
live in cities

People Today

live in the 2000s
modern cities
have televisions

Talk About It Look at the organizer. Complete the sentences below with a partner.

Both the Aztecs and people today _____.

Unlike people today, the Aztecs _____.

Your Turn Look at the passage on page 159. Write two sentences that compare or contrast the city Cortés explored to a city you know.

_____

_____

_____

Comparative and Superlative Adjectives

Adjectives describe people or things.

Comparative adjectives often end in *-er.*

Superlative adjectives often end in *-est.*

big

bigger

biggest

Talk About It Use adjectives with *-er* and *-est* in the following sentences.

The ancient city was the _____ and most beautiful city the men had ever seen. (large)

Cortés's expedition was _____ and more violent than anyone expected. (long)

Your Turn Write two sentences with *-er* and *-est* adjectives. Tell about the size of something you see in the classroom.

_____

_____

_____

Think, Talk, and Write

Ancient Civilizations Think about the ancient Aztecs in Mexico. Today scholars go on expeditions to find out about ancient cultures. Sometimes they find surprising things.

What might surprise scholars about the ancient Greeks?

What might surprise scholars about the ancient Egyptians?

Talk About It Review the vocabulary on page 158. Work with a partner to tell about each word. Which words will you use to write a story about an expedition to an ancient civilization?

Produce Language Write a story about an expedition to an ancient civilization. First complete the chart. Then write 4 to 5 sentences in your Weekly Concept Journal.

My ancient civilization: _____

_____

What happened in the expedition: _____

_____

What was surprising: _____

_____

Vocabulary words I can use: _____

_____

Heroism

Vocabulary

coil

ridge

confidently
hero
nervously
trekked
void

What does it take to be a hero?

A hero may bravely save someone's life on a mountain. A hero may quietly help a student at school. If you look carefully around you, you will probably find heroes. You might even be someone's hero!

Vocabulary in Context

Read the passage together.
Then circle the vocabulary words.

An Unexpected Hero

Angelina and Judy trekked along the mountain ridge. They looked down nervously at the deep void below them. They were experienced hikers, but they could fall if they were not careful.

Suddenly Judy screamed as part of the ridge broke away. She fell, but she slipped only twenty feet down.

"Don't worry, Judy. I've got you," Angelina called confidently.

She threw a coil of rope down to Judy. Judy tied it tightly around her. Angelina tied the other end of the rope to a tree. Then Judy climbed slowly up the cliff.

"You rescued me!" Judy exclaimed. "You are my hero!"

Talk About It What makes a person a hero? Complete the sentences below.

A hero is someone who _____ .

Angelina is a hero because she _____ .

Your Turn There are many ways to be a hero. What heroes can you think of? Have you ever met a hero? Tell a partner your thoughts about heroes.

Describing We use words to describe things. Words such as *might* and *could* tell about things that have not yet happened. They show that we think those things are possible.

Examples:

> I think that the women **might** finish the hike successfully and return home happily afterward.
>
> After the hike, the women **could** get a snack.

. . . .

Talk About It Tell a partner about a hero of yours. What could that hero do?

> My hero _____ could _____ .

. . . .

Your Turn Write a sentence that describes something another hero might do.

_____

_____

_____

_____

Plot and Setting A story is made up of events in the order in which they happen. These events are the **plot** of the story. The **setting** is where and when the story takes place.

Fill in the blank space with an action a hero could take in a city.

Setting	Plot
mountain	rescuing someone who fell
ocean	rescuing someone who can't swim
city	

- -

Talk About It What events make up the plot of "An Unexpected Hero"?

Complete the sentences below with a partner.

Angelina rescues Judy because _____.

In the future, Angelina and Judy might _____.

- -

Your Turn Write a sentence that describes the setting of the passage on page 165. Then write a sentence that describes what you think might happen next in the plot of the story.

_____

_____

_____

_____

Grammar

Adverbs When we talk about an action, we want to describe it. An **adverb** is a word that describes an action. Many adverbs end in *-ly,* such as *bravely* and *horribly.* You can combine adverbs in sentences. The adverbs are circled in the chart below.

| Angelina acted bravely. | Angelina acted calmly. | Angelina acted bravely and calmly. |

Talk About It Complete the sentences below with a partner. Use adverbs in your sentences.

The doctor _____ helps the girl feel better.

The firefighters _____ stop the fire.

Your Turn Use adverbs to complete the sentences below. Then use an adverb to write a sentence of your own.

The hero climbed _____ down the mountain.

Heroes act _____ and _____ .

_____

_____

Think, Talk, and Write

Heroism Think about how Judy called Angelina her hero. Talk with a partner about other ways you can express thanks to your hero.

Can your teacher be a hero?

Can your brother be a hero?

Talk About It Review the vocabulary on page 164. Work with a partner to tell about each word. Which words will you use to write about your hero?

Produce Language Write a poem about someone who is your hero. First complete the chart. Then write 4 to 5 sentences in your Weekly Concept Journal.

My hero: _____

_____

Words to describe my hero: _____

_____

Why the person is my hero: _____

_____

Vocabulary words I can use: _____

_____

Vocabulary

explorers

scientists

anticipation

faced

sacrifice

unknown

What does a person sacrifice to explore the unknown?

To explore the unknown parts of the world, you would have to sacrifice many things. Television, cars, and computers would have to be left behind. You would also have to sacrifice spending time with your family and friends.

Read the passage together.
Then circle the vocabulary words.

Exploring the Arctic

People sacrifice a great deal to travel to the Arctic. They have left behind family and friends in anticipation of finding out more about the Arctic.

The Arctic is the land that is farthest north on Earth. It has very low temperatures, harsh winds, and thick ice. The first explorers to the Arctic traveled many miles by boat. Some did not even reach the Arctic. Those who did reach the Arctic had faced the unknown. They found it hard to survive.

Today, scientists and others still explore the Arctic. They want to find out more about the land and the plants and animals that live there. New kinds of travel and weather-proofed buildings make it easier to explore the Arctic, but it is still hard to survive there.

Talk About It What would you have to sacrifice to explore the Arctic? Complete the sentences below.

Traveling to the Arctic would be _____ because _____.

To explore there, you would have to _____.

Your Turn Would you sacrifice something to go to the Arctic? Why or why not? Tell a partner.

Summarizing We use words to summarize. To summarize is to tell the main points of what you read, see, or hear. You might use phrases such as *in short, in summary,* or *indeed* to sum up ideas.

Circle the summarizing words in the sentences below.

In summary,	In summary, the desert explorer was happy he made sacrifices to explore the desert.
In short,	In short, people who explore do have to make sacrifices.
Indeed,	Indeed, the astronaut felt that it was difficult to leave family and friends behind.

. . . .

Talk About It What have you learned about making sacrifices? Summarize for a partner.

In short, _____ .

. . . .

Your Turn Would you make sacrifices to explore a new place? Summarize your feelings below. Use words from the chart.

_____

_____

_____

Main Idea/Details The **main idea** is the most important idea in the text. Sometimes it includes summary words, such as *in short* or *in summary*. **Details** are facts that help you understand the main idea.

The main idea is the last sentence in the paragraph below. Circle the details.

Some explorers travel to space. Some people explore deserts or rainforests. Others explore icy lands, such as the Arctic. In short, there are many ways people explore the unknown.

Talk About It Talk with a partner about the paragraph above. Complete the sentences below with a partner.

The main idea is that _____.

One supporting fact is that _____.

Your Turn Look at the passage on page 171. Complete the chart with details from the passage.

Main Idea: The first explorers had to sacrifice to explore the Arctic.		
They had to _____ _____ _____	**They had to** _____ _____ _____	**They had to** _____ _____ _____

Comparative and Superlative Adverbs A word that describes an action is called an **adverb.** The **comparative** form usually ends in *-er* or has the word *more* in front. The **superlative** form usually ends in *-est* or has the word *most* in front.

Adverb	Comparative Form	Superlative Form
quickly	more quickly	most quickly
slowly	more slowly	most slowly
fast	faster	fastest

Talk About It Read the sentences and circle the comparative and superlative adverbs.

Hal's dogs are running more slowly than Jim's.

The bear on the left runs faster than the bear on the right.

Your Turn Finish the sentences. Use adverbs from the chart. Then use an adverb to write a sentence of your own.

Marta built her igloo _____ than Felicia.

Nguyen trains dogs the _____ .

_____

_____

Think, Talk, and Write

Adaptations to Harsh Climates Think about how Arctic explorers must adapt to the cold to survive. Talk with a partner about other places that have harsh climates.

How is a desert climate harsh?

How is a wet, rainy climate harsh?

Talk About It Review the vocabulary on page 170. Work with a partner to tell about each word. Which words will you use to write about a harsh climate you want to explore?

Produce Language Write about a place with a harsh climate that you would like to explore. First complete the chart. Then write 4 to 5 sentences in your Weekly Concept Journal.

My harsh climate: _____

_____

My sacrifice: _____

_____

What I would explore: _____

_____

Vocabulary words I can use: _____

_____

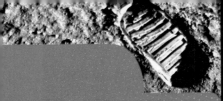

The Moon

What are the risks when walking on the moon?

In 1969, the first person walked on the moon. Astronauts were not sure exactly what they would find on the moon. They needed spacesuits to breathe. They had to spend more than 100 hours traveling on a spacecraft. But astronauts were glad to take the risk.

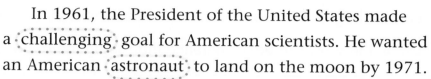

Read the passage together.
Then circle the vocabulary words.

The First Walk on the Moon

In 1961, the President of the United States made a challenging goal for American scientists. He wanted an American astronaut to land on the moon by 1971.

Scientists worked hard as the deadline loomed. It was a risk. No one had landed on the moon before. No one knew what to expect.

On July 20, 1969, astronaut Neil Armstrong left his spacecraft and bravely walked on the moon's surface. The moon has very little gravity. This made Armstrong seem weightless, but he did not float into space. The first walk on the moon was a success. Armstrong said the first walk on the moon was a "leap for mankind."

. . . .

Talk About It What happened on the first walk on the moon? Complete the sentences below.

> The first walk on the moon was a risk because _____ .
>
> Neil Armstrong was _____ .
>
> The first walk on the moon was _____ .

. . . .

Your Turn What do you think it would be like to walk on the moon? Tell a partner.

Literary Analysis We can use complex sentences to describe things. Complex sentences have two parts, or clauses. Both clauses have verbs, but only one clause can stand alone. This is the independent clause. The clause that cannot stand alone is called the dependent clause. Dependent clauses begin with words such as *when, because, if,* and *that.*

Circle the words in each sentence that begin the dependent clause.

Dependent	Independent	Sentence
When the astronauts landed on the moon	they did not know what to expect.	When the astronauts landed on the moon, they did not know what to expect.
because there is no gravity on the moon.	The astronauts felt weightless	The astronauts felt weightless because there is no gravity on the moon.
if I could walk on the moon.	I would take a risk	I would take a risk if I could walk on the moon.

Talk About It Read these complex sentences with a partner. Tell which parts of the sentences can stand alone.

The astronaut could breathe on the moon because he was wearing a spacesuit.

When the astronaut walked on the moon, he left footprints.

Your Turn Write a complex sentence using *that* or *if.* Circle the part of your sentence that cannot stand alone.

_____

_____

Character/Setting The people or animals in a story are the **characters.** The time and place in which the story occurs is called the **setting.**

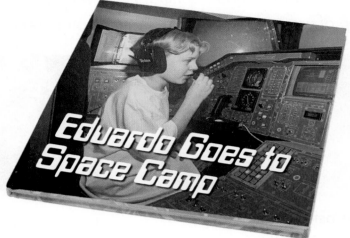

Eduardo Goes to Space Camp

Talk About It Look at the book above. From the picture and the title, what can you learn about "Eduardo Goes to Space Camp"?

Complete the sentence below with a partner.

> The character is _____.
>
> The setting is _____.

Your Turn Write a sentence that tells about a character you have read about. Use *that* or *because* if you can.

_____

_____

_____

Prepositions and Prepositional Phrases A **preposition** is a word that relates a noun or pronoun to another word in the sentence. The words *in, beside, under, behind, near, with, at, on, at the bottom of,* and *on top of* are examples of prepositions, and prepositional phrases.

The astronaut is
:beside: the flag.

The astronaut is
:on top of: the bar.

Talk About It Read the sentences and circle the prepositions. Tell a partner.

The astronaut is
on the moon.

Astronauts travel
in a spaceship.

Your Turn Finish the sentences. Use prepositions from the list above.

The astronauts floated _____ each other.

The spaceship flew _____ the earth.

Think, Talk, and Write

The Moon Think about the risk Neil Armstrong took when he walked on the moon in 1969. Talk with a partner about the other risks of space travel.

What are the risks during liftoff?   What are the risks during flight?

- -

Talk About It Review the vocabulary on page 176. Work with a partner to tell about each word. Which words will you use to write about the reasons why you would travel to the moon?

- -

Produce Language Write about the reasons why you would travel to the moon. First complete the chart. Then write 4 to 5 sentences in your Weekly Concept Journal.

My trip to the moon: _____

_____

Reasons for traveling: _____

_____

The risks of traveling: _____

_____

Vocabulary words I can use: _____

_____

Get Online!

Hear it!
See it!
Do it!

- Big Question Video
- Concept Talk Video
- Envision It! Animation
- Grammar Jammer

Reaching For Goals

 What does it take to achieve our goals and dreams?

Unit 6

Equal Opportunities
How can words change people's lives?

Challenges
How can our abilities influence our dreams and goals?

Coming to a New Culture
How can one person's view of the world affect others?

Achieving Goals
What can people do to achieve their goals?

Space Exploration
How do the achievements of others influence our dreams?

Reaching for Goals

Equal Opportunities

Vocabulary

pump

sign language

avoided
eyesight
importance
numerous

How can words change people's lives?

People use words to communicate with each other. We speak, hear, and read words. In general, words cannot be avoided— they are an important part of our lives.

Read the passage together.
Then circle the vocabulary words.

The Story of Helen Keller

Helen Keller was a famous blind and deaf woman. She lost her eyesight and her hearing when she was a baby.

Helen Keller had a teacher named Anne Sullivan. At first Sullivan tried to teach Keller numerous words. She used sign language, but Keller did not understand. Then one day, Sullivan held Keller's hand under a water pump. Keller felt the water. Sullivan spelled w-a-t-e-r in Keller's hand. Finally Keller understood! Keller tapped the ground. Sullivan spelled e-a-r-t-h.

When Helen Keller grew up, she wrote books and spoke to people. She helped people understand the importance of words.

- -

Talk About It Why were words important to Helen Keller? Talk with a partner. Use the sentence frames below.

> Helen Keller was _____.
>
> Anne Sullivan taught Keller _____.
>
> Keller knew how important it was for people to _____.

- -

Your Turn What were the first English words you learned? How did they help you?

My first English words were _____.

They helped me because _____.

FORM & FUNCTION

Cause-and-Effect Relationship We can use past tense verbs, such as *walked* or *said,* to tell about things that happened in the past. Many of these words end in *-ed.* These words can help us tell about cause and effect. A **cause** is why something happens. An **effect** is what happens.

Example: Maya **understood** her teacher, so she **learned** words.

Circle the words that show past tense.

I can speak two languages because I studied very hard.

Jason loved school because he learned new things.

Anne worked very hard, so she became a good teacher.

. . . .

Talk About It Say a sentence that uses the past tense of *learn.*

. . . .

Your Turn Write a sentence below. Use a past tense verb, such as *worked.*

_____

_____

Cause and Effect Many stories and articles tell about causes and effects. A **cause** is why something happens. An **effect** is what happens. Clue words such as *because, so,* and *since* tell about cause and effect.

Cause   **Clue Word**   **Effect**

Example: (Tim studied very hard), **so** (he learned a lot of new vocabulary words).

- -

Talk About It Read each sentence with a partner.
Circle the effect. Underline the cause.

> Tim gave a good speech, so he was voted class leader.
>
> Rosa was very happy because she gave a good speech.

- -

Your Turn Look at the passage on page 185. What caused Helen Keller to learn words? Write the cause and effect. Use the word *because.*

_____

_____

_____

Conjunctions We use **conjunctions** to connect words or the parts of sentences. The words *and, or, but,* and *yet* are conjunctions. These conjunctions join sentence parts that are equally important.

Maria (and) Judy went to the library today.

The library was open, (but) it was not crowded.

Laurie will write a letter (or) a postcard.

• •

Talk About It What are the conjunctions in these sentences? Tell a partner.

Mr. Jenkins and Tyler read stories aloud.

Masha and Dan can read aloud or silently to themselves.

• •

Your Turn Circle each conjunction. Draw a line under the sentence parts the conjunctions join together.

Todd read a book and a magazine over the weekend.

Sara read the story quickly, but she understood it.

Would you like to read a book or listen to a speech?

Think, Talk, and Write

Equal Opportunities Think about how Helen Keller learned the importance of words from her teacher, Anne Sullivan. Talk with a partner about how words give people opportunities.

How do words on television give people opportunities?

How do Braille words give people opportunities?

Talk About It Review the vocabulary on page 184. Work with a partner to tell about each word. Which words will you use to write about why it is important to communicate with others?

Produce Language Write about a time when words gave you an opportunity to help others. First complete the chart. Then write 4 to 5 sentences in your Weekly Concept Journal.

What I communicated: _____

_____

Words I used when I communicated: _____

_____

Why it was important: _____

_____

Vocabulary words I can use in my writing: _____

_____

Vocabulary

champion

medal

ability
disease
endurance
goal
rejected
society

How can our abilities influence our dreams and goals?

An ability is a talent or a skill. We all have abilities. We can use our abilities to work toward and achieve our dreams and goals.

Read the passage together.
Then circle the vocabulary words.

The Story of an Athlete

As a child, Wilma Rudolph had a (disease) called polio. Doctors told Rudolph's mother that Rudolph would never walk.

Rudolph's mother (rejected) the doctor's words. Rudolph also did not give up, and she began to walk.

Rudolph soon found that she had a natural ability for sports. She worked hard at running. At age 16, she became a track champion. She went to the Olympics in 1956 and won a bronze medal. At the 1960 Olympics, she won three gold medals. Rudolph showed society that ability and endurance can help a person achieve a goal.

. . . .

Talk About It Why did Rudolph become a great athlete? Complete the sentences below.

As a child, Rudolph _____ .

Rudolph _____ , and she eventually won a medal at the Olympics.

Rudolph's abilities led her to win many _____ and to become a truly great _____ .

. . . .

Your Turn Think about your abilities. What goals can you make based on your abilities?

One ability I have is _____ .

My goal is to _____ .

191

FORM & FUNCTION

Comparing We use words ending in *-er* and *-est* to compare things.

Example: Sue is the **fastest** runner in the class.
Sam was a **faster** runner than his brother.

The chart below shows some words that compare.

fast	faster	fastest
large	larger	largest
small	smaller	smallest
bright	brighter	brightest
happy	happier	happiest

Circle the words that compare in the sentences below.

Robinson practices harder at playing piano than Jill.

Wilma was the fastest track star at the games.

Yin was happier than Tom when the class won the spelling bee.

· ·

Talk About It Say a sentence that compares two things.
Use one of the words in the chart.

· ·

Your Turn Look at the picture.
Write a sentence that compares
the runners in the picture. Use
words that compare and contrast.

_____

_____

Compare and Contrast To **compare** is to tell how things are alike. To **contrast** is to tell how things are different. When we read, we can compare and contrast. We can use words that end in *-er* and *-est* to help compare.

Circle the words in the captions that compare and contrast.

Rhonda kicks the ball farther than most players.

Jason jumps higher than his teammates.

. . . .

Talk About It Look at the pictures. What can you tell about these athletes? Complete the sentences below.

Rhonda and Jason are alike because _____ .

Rhonda and Jason are different because _____ .

. . . .

Your Turn Reread the passage on page 191. How was Wilma Rudolph like other athletes? How was she different? Use *-er* and *-est* words.

_____

_____

_____

Capitalization Letters are written in two ways. *G* is a **capital letter.** This is also called an uppercase letter. *G* is written *g* in lowercase. A capital letter is always used at the beginning of a sentence.

The sentences below show some uses of capital letters. Names of magazines, newspapers, songs, and art should be capitalized. Look at the examples circled below.

I read *the (L)os (A)ngeles (T)imes* today.

Do you know the words to the song "(T)hree (B)lind (M)ice"?

Picasso's *(T)he (O)ld (G)uitarist* is my favorite painting.

Talk About It Which words should be capitalized? Explain.

mona lisa

"america the beautiful"

Your Turn Write a sentence telling about a magazine or a song you know. Use correct capitalization.

_____

_____

Think, Talk, and Write

Challenges Think about how Wilma Rudolph overcame polio and went on to be a champion. Talk with a partner about other people who have used their abilities to achieve goals.

How did Lance Armstrong overcome a challenge?

How did Terry Fox overcome a challenge?

Talk About It Review the vocabulary on page 190. Work with a partner to tell about each word. Which words will you use to write about a famous person who has achieved his or her goals?

Produce Language Write about a famous person who has achieved his or her goals. First complete the chart. Then write 4 to 5 sentences in your Weekly Concept Journal.

My person's ability: _____

_____

My person's challenge: _____

_____

How he or she achieved a goal: _____

_____

Vocabulary words I can use: _____

_____

Vocabulary

PICTURE IT!

palettes

PICTURE IT!

plantains

quaint

realistic

self-portraits

unusual

How can one person's view of the world affect others?

People have different views of the world. Sometimes a person's view can affect the way others think and feel. A person's view can also affect what we do and even change our lives.

Read the passage together.
Then circle the vocabulary words.

The New Girl

My friend Dora moved from South America to our quaint town last year. She speaks Spanish and English. She brings us South American snacks. Her grilled plantains seemed unusual at first. But they were delicious!

Dora taught me something in art class one day. My self-portraits never looked realistic. I couldn't make the colors from the palettes look natural on paper. But Dora didn't worry about whether her picture seemed real. Instead she painted her picture with bright colors. Her painting was beautiful.

I realized then that art didn't have to be about what you see with your eyes. Art can be about what you see with your heart.

Talk About It How did Dora affect other people? Complete the sentences below.

Dora taught others _____.

Dora is _____.

Your Turn What can you learn from someone from another country? How could he or she affect you? Tell a partner.

Evaluating We use words to evaluate, or to judge, something. When we evaluate, we use certain words to tell our views about something. We use words such as *think* and *feel* when we evaluate.

The chart shows some words that are used to evaluate.

think	feel	believe
don't think	certain	sure
likely	probably	unsure

Circle the words in the sentences below that show thinking and feeling.

I am certain many people will like this painting.

I believe that Dora's classmate learned to like painting more.

Talk About It Look at the photograph below.
What do you think the man in the photograph is feeling? Why?
Complete the sentence below. Say your sentence to a partner.

I think the soccer player _____
because he _____ .

Your Turn Write a sentence that evaluates.
Tell what you think or feel about a song or painting.

_____

_____

Character and Theme The people or animals in a story are the **characters.** The **theme** is the meaning, or big idea, of a story. We can use words that evaluate to tell about the characters and theme of a story.

Dora is the main character in "The New Girl" on page 197. The story focuses on her. Her actions give the story meaning.

Talk About It Look at the story you read on page 197.

Complete each sentence below. Say your sentences to a partner.

I think the theme of the story is _____ .

I feel this way because _____ .

Your Turn Look at the passage on page 197. Write a sentence about the character Dora. Include words that evaluate.

_____

_____

Commas You know that a sentence begins with a capital letter and ends with a period. A **comma** shows a pause in a sentence. Some sentences, called quotations, show the words that characters speak. A comma is often used at the end of a quotation before the quotation mark.

"I think it is important to try tamales," said Roy.

comma

"Let's try the new South American restaurant," said Dawn.

comma

Talk About It Where does a comma belong in each sentence? Talk with a partner about where the commas belong.

"I never knew South American food was so good" said Roy.

"This rice dish is excellent" said Dawn.

Your Turn Read each sentence below and add a comma to each one.

"Mr. Ray is the best art teacher we've ever had" said Jason.

"I think so too" said Luis.

"He makes art class fun" said Ali.

Coming to a New Culture Think about how Dora must have felt when she moved from South America. Talk with a partner about what Dora's view of the United States might have been.

How does an American artist view the Pacific Ocean?

How does a Mexican artist view the Pacific Ocean?

Talk About It Review the vocabulary on page 196. Work with a partner to tell about each word. Which words will you use to write about a character whose view affects others?

Produce Language Write a story that tells how the character's view of the world affects others. First complete the chart. Then write 4 to 5 sentences in your Weekly Concept Journal.

My character: _____

_____

My character's view: _____

_____

How the view affects others: _____

_____

Vocabulary words I can use: _____

_____

Vocabulary

PICTURE IT!

field

PICTURE IT!

practice

assignment

fortitude

improve

rumor

What can people do to achieve their goals?

With hard work, we can achieve, or reach, our goals. A goal might be something that a person achieves, such as becoming a better soccer player.

Read the passage together.
Then circle the vocabulary words.

On the Field

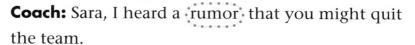

Scene: A soccer field in a park

Coach: Sara, I heard a rumor that you might quit the team.

Sara: I love soccer, Coach, but I'm just not good at kicking the ball where I want it to go. My goal was to be a great player, but it's too hard.

Coach: Sometimes achieving goals is difficult, but you have to have fortitude and keep trying. You can improve all your skills.

Sara: But what can I do to improve?

Coach: Start small. Here's your assignment for tonight: Practice kicking the ball against the wall. You'll improve in no time if you do a little extra work each night.

Sara: Great idea, Coach! I'll get started right away!

• •

Talk About It What does Sara need to do to achieve her goal of becoming a better player? Complete the sentences below.

Sara wants to _____.

Sara will achieve her goal by _____.

• •

Your Turn What goal would you like to achieve? How will you reach your goal? Tell a partner.

Describing We use words to describe events and actions. When we describe events and the actions of characters in a story, we can use words to tell how, where, or when. We can use words that answer the question *when?* to tell when the next soccer game will be.

Example: The next soccer game is **on Friday.**

Circle the word or words in each sentence that tell how, where, or when.

How?	I am learning to play as skillfully as Mia Hamm.
Where?	I practice shooting goals at the field on the school playground.
When?	We will go out to eat after the game.

Talk About It Say sentences that describe how, where, and when you might practice a sport or other skill.

Complete the sentences.

I will practice by _____ .

I will practice at _____ .

I will practice after _____ .

Your Turn Write a sentence that describes what a boy in the picture is doing. Include words that tell how, when, or where.

_____

_____

Character and Plot Stories have **characters** and events. A **plot** is the important events of a story. A plot has a beginning, a middle, and an end. The plot centers around the characters in the story. We can use words that describe how, when, and where to talk about characters and plot. The diagram below shows the parts of a plot.

A Plot Diagram

Climax
Mrs. Kim offers to teach Joe piano after school.

Problem
Joe wants to learn piano, but he does not have money for lessons.

Outcome
At last, Joe is learning to play piano skillfully.

Talk About It Look at the plot diagram above. Who is the main character? What is the climax, or highpoint, of this plot? Use words that describe how, when, and where.

Complete the sentences below.

> The main character is _____. He has a problem because _____.
>
> Another character decides to _____.

Your Turn Read the play on page 203. Think about the characters and plot. What is the problem? How is it solved?

_____

_____

Quotations and Quotation Marks A **quotation** is a person's words that are repeated by another person. The first word in a quotation is usually a capital letter. Some sentences in a story show the words that characters speak. These sentences are set off with **quotation marks.**

Quotation	Quotation Marks
"I play to win, whether during practice or a real game." –Michael Jordan	"I would like to be a great ball player one day," said Angela. "If you work hard, you can do it!" said Denny.

Talk About It Which parts of the sentences need quotation marks? Tell how you know.

Just play. Have fun. Enjoy the game.

–Michael Jordan

Would you like to learn to catch a baseball? asked John.

Your Turn Where are quotation marks needed? Write the quotation marks in the proper places.

Would you like to become a great ball player? asked Jack.

The game is my life. –Michael Jordan

Think, Talk, and Write

Achieving Goals Think about how Sara tried to reach her goal of being a great soccer player. Talk with a partner about things people can do to achieve their goals.

Will shooting hoops help her play better?

Will lifting weights help him run faster?

Talk About It Review the vocabulary on page 202. Work with a partner to tell about each word. Which words will you use to write about what people do to achieve their goals?

Produce Language Write about a goal you have and the steps you can take to achieve it. First complete the chart. Then write 4 to 5 sentences in your Weekly Concept Journal.

My goal: _____

_____

First step: _____

_____

Next step: _____

_____

Vocabulary words I can use: _____

_____

Vocabulary

PICTURE IT!

capsule

PICTURE IT!

hatch

achievements

inspired

orbit

How do the achievements of others influence our dreams?

An achievement is something special that a person has done. In the early 1960s, the achievements of a group of astronauts led the way for others to explore space.

Read the passage together.
Then circle the vocabulary words.

THE FIRST ASTRONAUTS

On May 5, 1961, astronaut Alan Shepard was blasting his way into space. About 15 minutes later, his space capsule splashed down in the Atlantic Ocean. Shepard crawled out through the capsule's hatch with a huge smile. For him, this first-ever U.S. space flight was a dream come true.

The next year, on February 20, 1962, John Glenn also went into space. He was the first American astronaut to orbit, or travel around, Earth in space. His spacecraft, called *Friendship 7*, returned to Earth after nearly five hours. These early space flights made history. The astronauts' achievements inspired other astronauts who later walked on the moon!

Talk About It What did the first astronauts achieve? Complete the sentences below.

> Alan Shepard was the first American astronaut to _____ .
>
> John Glenn was the first American astronaut to _____ .

Your Turn How did the achievements of these early astronauts affect other astronauts? Tell a partner.

Describing We use words to describe things. When we describe things that happen, we often include where they take place.

Example: The early space capsules landed **in the ocean.**

We can use words to answer the question *where?*
to tell about where things take place.

Circle the words to answer the question *where?* in each sentence below.

around	John Glenn's spacecraft orbited around Earth.
outside	The name *Friendship 7* is on the outside of the capsule.
inside	The astronaut sits inside of the space capsule.
on top of	The space capsule floats on top of the waves.

Talk About It Say a sentence to describe the astronaut in this picture. Include words that describe where.

Your Turn Write a sentence to describe the astronaut in the picture. Include words that describe where.

_____

_____

Graphic Sources **Graphic sources** give information using words and pictures. A chart is a graphic source. A photograph is a graphic source. A diagram is a graphic source. Diagrams have labels to describe their parts. Graphic sources can be used to describe where something is.

Circle the labels on the diagram for the Mercury Space Capsule.

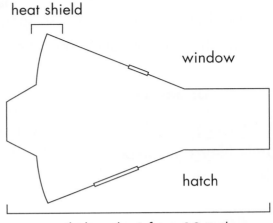

Mercury Space Capsule

heat shield

window

hatch

capsule length: 6 feet, 10 inches

Talk About It Look at the graphic source of the Mercury Space Capsule. What information does the graphic source give you about space capsules?

Complete the sentences below.

A space capsule has _____ and _____ .

Inside the capsule, the astronaut _____ .

Your Turn Look at this chart. What information does the chart tell you?

Write a sentence below that tells something you learned.

Astronaut	Capsule	Length of Flight
Alan Shepard	*Freedom 7*	15 min 28 sec
John Glenn	*Friendship 7*	4 hours 55 min

Titles A **title** can be the name of a book, a song, or a poem. There are different ways to write titles. <u>Underline</u> the title of a book, magazine, or newspaper. Use quotation marks to write the titles of songs and poems.

Underline	Quotation Marks
<u>All About Space</u> (Book) <u>Daily News</u> (Newspaper)	"When I'm an Astronaut" (Poem) "Star-Spangled Banner" (Song)

- -

Talk About It Should you use an underline or quotation marks to write each title?

Astronaut Achievements

New York Times

- -

Your Turn Write the title. Use either an underline or quotation marks.

Exploring Space (Book) _____

The Road Not Taken (Poem) _____

Lost in Space (Song) _____

Chicago Tribune (Newspaper) _____

Think, Talk, and Write

Space Exploration Think about how Alan Shepard's space flight inspired others to become astronauts. Talk with a partner about how astronauts' achievements inspire others.

How can Space Camp inspire us?

How can the Space Station inspire us?

- -

Talk About It Review the vocabulary on page 208. Work with a partner to tell about each word. Which words will you use to write about something that inspired you?

- -

Produce Language Write about someone or something that inspires you. First complete the chart. Then write 4 to 5 sentences in your Weekly Concept Journal.

My inspiration: _____

_____

What I can achieve: _____

_____

My goals: _____

_____

Vocabulary words I can use: _____

_____

Glossary

How to Use This Glossary

This glossary can help you understand and pronounce some of the words in this book. The words at the top of each page show the first and last words on the page. The pronunciation key is on page 215. Remember, if you can't find the word you are looking for, ask for help or check a dictionary.

The entry word is in dark type. It shows how the word is spelled.

The pronunciation is in parentheses. It also shows which syllables are stressed.

Part-of-speech labels show the function of the word.

adapt (ə dapt′), *v.* to change your behavior or ideas to fit a new situation

Aa

ability (ə bil′ə tē), *N.* a talent or skill

abolitionists (ab′ə lish′ə nists), *N.* people who supported the end of slavery

achieve (ə chēv′), *v.* to succeed in getting a good result in doing something you want

achievements (ə chēv′mənts), *N.* successes in doing or getting what you worked for

ancient (ān′shənt), *ADJ.* belonging to a time thousands of years ago

anticipation (an tis′ə pā′shən), *N.* a feeling of excitement for something that is going to happen

anticrime (an′tī krīm′), *ADJ.* against illegal activities

appreciate (ə prē′shē āt), *v.* to understand the good qualities or value of something

aquatic (ə kwat′ik), *ADJ.* living or happening in water

argument (är′gyə mənt), *N.* a disagreement

arrangements (ə rānj′mənts), *N.* plans or preparations to be ready for something

assembly line (ə sem′blē līn), *N.* a system for making things in which workers each make one part of the product

assignment (ə sīn′mənt), *N.* a piece of work that is given to someone

assistant (ə sis′ tənt), *N.* someone whose job is to help another worker

astronaut (as′trə nȯt), *N.* someone who travels into space

athletes (ath′lētz), *N.* those who are good at sports or who often play sports

attention (ə ten′shən), *N.* careful observation or watching of things or persons

audience (ȯ′dē əns), *N.* a group of people who listen to or watch a show

autumn (ȯ′təm), *N.* one of the four seasons

avoided (ə void′ed), *v.* deliberately stayed away from someone or something

Bb

banjo (ban′jō), *N.* a musical instrument with strings

behave (bi hāv′), *v.* to do or say things in a particular way

biologists (bī ol′əjsts), *N.* people who study living things; a kind of scientist

blind (blīnd), *ADJ.* unable to see

brilliant (bril′yənt), *ADJ.* bright and strong

Cc

cactus (kak′təs), *N.* a desert plant

214

cannery (kan′ər ē), N. a factory or place where food is put into cans

capital (kap′ə təl), N. the city where a country's or state's main government is

capsule (kap′səl), N. the part of a spacecraft in which people live and work

challenge (chal′ənj), N. a test of skill or ability

challenging (chal′ənj ing), ADJ. testing your skill or ability

champion (cham′pē ən), N. a person or team that has won a competition

citizens (sit′ə zənz), N. people who live in a particular town, state, or country

cliffs (klifs), N. large areas of tall rocks

climates (klī′mits), N. the typical weather conditions in an area

coil (koil), N. a grouping of circles, like on a spring

communicate (kə myü′nə kāt), V. to exchange information using sounds or signs

compete (kəm pēt′), V. to try to win something

confidently (kon′fə dənt′lē), ADV. with the understanding that one can do things well

conveyor belt (kən vā′ər belt), N. a long, continuous moving band of rubber or metal that is used to move things

countless (kount′lis), ADJ. very many

cowboy (kou′boi′), N. a man who rides horses and takes care of cattle

coyote (kī ō′tē), N. a dog-like wild animal that lives in western North America and Mexico

crime (krīm), N. illegal activities

culture (kul′chər), N. the art, beliefs, behavior, or ideas of a particular group of people

Dd

dangerous (dān′jər əs), ADJ. likely to harm

decisions (di sizh′ənz), N. choices that a person makes

delights (di līts′), N. feelings of great pleasure

desert (dez′ərt), N. a large area of land where it is hot and dry

destroyed (di stroid′), V. damaged so badly that it cannot be used or it no longer exists

destruction (di struk′shən), N. damage

details (dē′tāls), N. pieces of information

detective (di tek′tiv), N. a kind of police officer who solves crimes

diamond (dī′mənd), N. a valuable jewel

discovered (dis kuv′ərd), V. saw or learned something new

disease (də zēz′), N. a sickness or illness

distance (dis′təns) N. the amount of space between two places or things

distract (dis trakt′), V. to do something that takes attention away from something else

diverse (dī′vərs), ADJ. very different

Ee

emergency (i mer′jən sē), N. something unexpected and possibly dangerous

employment (em ploi′mənt), N. the state of having a job for which you earn money

a	in hat	ėr	in term	ô	in order	ch	in child	ə	= a in about
ā	in age	i	in it	oi	in oil	ng	in long	ə	= e in taken
â	in care	ī	in ice	ou	in out	sh	in she	ə	= i in pencil
ä	in far	o	in hot	u	in cup	th	in thin	ə	= o in lemon
e	in let	ō	in open	u̇	in put	ᴛʜ	in then	ə	= u in circus
ē	in equal	ȯ	in all	ü	in rule	zh	in measure		

enchanted (en chant′ed), *v.* fascinated by

endurance (en dür′əns), *N.* the ability to do something for a long time

enslaved (en slāvd′), *v.* forced by someone to work for little or no pay

escape (e skāp′), *v.* to get away

exhausting (eg zȯst′ing), *ADJ.* making extremely tired

expedition (ek′spə dish′ən), *N.* a long trip, often to a dangerous and unknown place

expensive (ek spen′siv), *ADJ.* costly

explorers (ek splôr′ərz), *N.* people who travel to new places

eyesight (ī′sīt′), *N.* the ability to see

Ff

faced (fāsd), *v.* dealt with a hard situation

fascinated (fas′n āt ed), *v.* interested

field (fēld), *N.* a place where sports are played

fingerprints (fing′gər prints′), *N.* marks made by the pattern of lines on the fingers

forecasts (fôr′kasts′), *N.* descriptions of what is likely to happen in the future

formation (fôr mā′shən), *N.* a particular shape or structure

fortitude (fôr′tə tüd), *N.* continued effort

fouled (fould), *v.* made mistakes that are against the rules of a game

frost (frȯst), *N.* white, powdery ice that covers things in cold weather

fundraiser (fund′rā′zər), *N.* an event to collect money for a specific purpose

funnel (fun′l), *N.* an open tube with a wide top and a narrow bottom

Gg

gleams (glēmz), *v.* shines brightly

glorious (glôr′ē əs), *ADJ.* extremely nice

goal (gōl), *N.* something that you hope to do in the future

gourd (gôrd), *N.* a large fruit with a hard shell that is sometimes used as a bowl

government (guv′ərn mənt), *N.* the group of people in charge of a country or state

gravity (grav′ə tē), *N.* the force that makes objects fall to the ground instead of floating up in the air

guide (gīd), *v.* to lead or show the way

Hh

habitat (hab′ə tat), *N.* the environment in which a plant or animal lives

harness (här′nis), *N.* leather bands used in order to control a horse

harsh (härsh), *ADJ.* difficult or unpleasant

hatch (hach), *N.* the door that covers a hole in a ship or aircraft

herd (hėrd), *N.* a group of a particular type of animal that lives together

hero (hir′ō), *N.* a brave person

hieroglyphics (hī′ər ə glif′iks), *N.* a system of writing with pictures instead of words

highway (hī′wā), *N.* a wide road

Ii

illusion (i lü′zhən), *N.* something that seems to be different from what it really is

immigrants (im′ə grənts), *N.* people who enter another country to live there

importance (im pôrt′ns), *N.* the quality of being important

impossible (im pos′ə bəl), *ADJ.* not correct or able to be done

impressive (im pres′iv), *ADJ.* very good

improve (im prüv′), *v.* to become better

independent (in′di pen′dənt), *ADJ.* able to take care of yourself without having help

inspired (in spīrd′), *v.* encouraged someone to do or produce something

Inuit (in′ü it), *N.* a group of people who live in Canada, Greenland, and Alaska

Ll

landscape (land′skāp), *N.* a view of an area of land, including hills, forests, and fields

lasso (las′ō), *N.* a rope with one end tied in a circle, used for catching cattle and horses

longed (lȯngd), *v.* wanted something

loomed (lümd), *v.* was likely to happen very soon

Mm

magician (mə jish′ən), *N.* someone who entertains people by doing magic tricks

mates (māts), *N.* partners

meadow (med′ō), *N.* a field with wild grass and flowers

medal (med′l), *N.* a piece of metal given to the winner of a competition

messages (mes′ij ez), *N.* spoken or written pieces of information sent to others

migrate (mīgrāt), *v.* to travel to a different part of the world when seasons change

migration (mī grā′shən), *N.* the action of a group of animals moving to a new area

mystery (mis′tər ē), *N.* something that is difficult to explain or understand

myth (mith), *N.* an ancient story

Nn

navigate (nav′ə gāt), *v.* to find one's way

nervously (nėr′vəs lē), *ADV.* in a worried way

numerous (nü′mər əs), *ADJ.* many

Oo

obstacle (ob′stə kəl), *N.* something that makes it difficult for you to succeed

official (ə fish′əl), *ADJ.* approved by someone in authority

opportunities (op′ər tü′nə tēz), *N.* times when it is possible to do something

orbit (ôr′bit), *v.* to travel in a circle around a larger object

Pp

palace (pal′lis), *N.* a very large house where a king or queen officially lives

palettes (pal′its), *N.* boards with a curved edge, on which painters mix colors

parachute (par′ə shüt), *N.* a large piece of cloth used to keep people safe when they jump out of airplanes

parlor (pär′lər), *N.* an old-fashioned name for a living room

pattern (pat′ərn), *N.* the repeated way in which something happens or is done

performing (pər form′ing), *v.* entertaining

pilot (pī′lət), *N.* someone who operates the controls of, or drives, an aircraft

plains (plānz), *N.* large areas of flat land

plantains (plan′tənz), *N.* large fruits that are somewhat like bananas

politics (pol′ə tiks), *N.* ideas and activities that are concerned with government

practice (prak′tis), *v.* to do a regular activity to improve a skill or ability

praises (prāz′ez), *N.* ways of showing appreciation for someone or something

preserve (pri zėrv′), *N.* a protected area

promoted (prə mōt′ ed), *v.* gave someone a better, more responsible position at work

protected (prə tekt′id), *v.* kept someone or something safe from harm

pump (pump), *N.* a machine that forces liquid into or out of something

Qq

quaint (kwānt), *ADJ.* unusual and attractive, especially in an old-fashioned way

Rr

radar (rā′där), *N.* equipment that uses radio waves to find the position of things

raised (rāzd), *v.* increased the amount

ranch (ranch), *N.* a very large farm where cattle, horses, or sheep are raised

realistic (rē′ə lis′tik), *ADJ.* looking the way it does in real life

refused (ri fyüzd′), *v.* did not agree

rejected (ri jekt′ed), *v.* did not accept

relieved (ri lēvd′), *ADJ.* no longer worried

rescue (res′kyü), *v.* to save someone or something from harm or danger

responsibility (ri spon′sə bil′ə tē), *N.* the state of being in charge of decisions

rickety (rik′ə tē), *ADJ.* in very bad condition

ridge (rij), *N.* a long area of high land

riverbed (riv′ər bed′), *N.* the ground over which a river flows

roadrunner (rōd′run′ər), *N.* a small bird in the Southwest that runs very fast

rotates (rō′tāts), *v.* turns around a point

route (rüt), *N.* the way from one place to another

ruins (rü′ənz), *N.* the parts of buildings that are left after the rest is damaged

rumor (rü′mər), *N.* information passed from one person to another that may not be true

Ss

sacrifice (sak′rə fis), *v.* to give up something

scholars (skol′ərz), *N.* those who know a lot about a particular subject

scientists (sī′ən tists), *N.* people who study science

sea level (sē lev′əl), *N.* the average level of the sea, used as a standard for measuring the height of an area of land

seasons (sē′zns), *N.* one of the four main weather periods in the year

self-portraits (self′pôr′trits), *N.* pictures that you make of yourself

sequoia (si kwoi′ə) *N.* a redwood tree

seriously (sir′ē əs lē) *ADV.* in a way that shows that something is important

service dog (sėr′vis dȯg) *N.* a dog that is trained to help people

shelter (shel′tər), *N.* a place that is protected from danger or the weather

sign language (sīn lang′gwij), *N.* a language that uses hands rather than spoken words

society (sə sī′ə tē), *N.* all the people who live together in a country or area

spacecraft (spās′kraft′), *N.* a vehicle that can travel in space

spacesuits (spās′sütz′), *N.* clothing that astronauts wear

speeches (spēch′ez), *N.* formal talks given to a group of people

station (stā′shən), *N.* a building or place that is a center for a type of activity

steer (stir), *v.* to control a vehicle

strayed (strād), *v.* wandered from the place where you should be

stumped (stumpt), *v.* unable to answer

supervisor (sü′pər vī′zər), N. someone who is in charge of other people or activities

surface (sėr′fis), N. the outside or top part of something

symbols (sim′bəlz), N. pictures or things that stand for, or mean, something else

Tt

talent (tal′ənt), N. a natural ability to do something well

teamwork (tēm′wėrk′), N. working well together to reach a goal

temperature (tem′pər ə chər), N. how hot or cold it is

tortoise (tôr′təs), N. a slow-moving animal with a hard shell that covers its body

towering (tou′ər ing), ADJ. very tall

traditional (trə dish′ə nəl), ADJ. describing methods that have existed for a long time

training (trā′ning), N. the process of teaching or being taught skills for a job

translate (trans′lāt), v. to change speech or writing from one language to another

transportation (tran′spər tā′shən), N. a system or method for carrying passengers or goods from one place to another

trekked (trekt), v. made a long and difficult trip, especially on foot

tropical (trop′ə kəl), ADJ. hot and wet

Uu

unbelievable (un′bi lē′və bəl), ADJ. not likely to be true

uniforms (yü′nə fôrmz), N. certain clothing that the members of a team wear

unique (yü nēk′), ADJ. unlike anything else

unknown (un nōn′), ADJ. not explored

unstable (un stā′bəl), ADJ. likely to change suddenly and become worse

untamed (un tāmd), ADJ. wild

unusual (un yü′zhü əl), ADJ. different from what is usual or normal

Vv

vast (vast), ADJ. extremely large

violent (vī′ə lənt), ADJ. strong and dangerous

void (void), N. an empty area of space

Ww

wages (wā′ jez), N. money paid for work

waterfall (wȯ′tər fȯl), N. water that falls straight down over a cliff

weightless (wāt′lis), ADJ. having no weight

White House (wīt hous), N. the home of the President of the United States

wilderness (wil′dər nis), N. a large area of land that has never been settled

Credits

Illustrations

25 Rick Drennan; 36, 130 Joe LeMonnier; 37 Doron Ben-Ami; 107 William Melvin

Photographs

Photo locators denoted as follows: Top (T), Center (C), Bottom (B), Left (L), Right (R), Background (Bkgd)

18 ©Randy Faris/Corbis; 23 Alamy Images, ©Rick Gomez/Corbis, ©Russ Bishop/Stock Connection/Jupiter Images, ©Daniel J. Cox/Getty Images; 24 (TL) Getty Images, (CL) ©Corbis Premium RF/Alamy, (BL) ©Hulton Archive/Stringer/Getty Images, (C) ©Robert Holmes/Corbis; 25 Judith Miller/Freeman's/DK Images; 26 ©Christina Kennedy/DK Stock/Getty Images; 27 ©Christine Robinson/Workbook Stock/Jupiter Images; 28 (BR) ©James Ross/Riser/Getty Images, (TR) ©DK Images; 29 (TL) Getty Images, (TR) ©Gallo Images/Stringer/Getty Images; 30 (TL) ©Genevieve Naylor/Corbis, (CL) ©Charles E. Rotkin/Corbis; 30 ©Fox Photos/Stringer/Hulton Archive/Getty Images; 31 Getty Images; 32 (TR) Jupiter Images, (CR) ©Dean Conger/Corbis, (BR) ©Ed Young/Corbis; 33 ©BLOOMimage/Getty Images; 34 (CL) ©Paul McMullin/Construction Photography, (CR) ©ColorBlind Images/Iconica/Getty Images; 35 (TR) ©redchopsticks/Getty Images, (TL) ©Scott Tysick/Masterfile Corporation; 36 (TL) ©Buddy Mays/Corbis, (BL) ©Jon Spaull/Dorling Kindersley/Getty Images, (CL) ©Susan E. Benson/Stock Connection, (C) ©Dale O'Dell/Omni Photo Communications; 37 ©Car Culture/Collection Mix: Subjects/Getty Images; 38 ©Bubbles Photolibrary/Alamy Images; 40 (BL) ©Andy Caulfield/Photographer's Choice/Getty Images, (CC) ©Justin Kase/Alamy, (CR) ©Atlantide Phototravel/Corbis, (TR) Getty Images; 41 Getty Images; 42 (TL) Getty Images, (CL) ©Theo Allofs/zefa/Corbis, (CL) ©Tom Vezo/Minden Pictures/Getty Images, (BL) ©DLILLC/Corbis; 43 ©George H. H. Huey/Corbis; 44 (BL) ©Ron Watts/Corbis, (TR) ©David Frazier/Corbis, (BR) ©David Muench/Corbis; 45 ©George H. H. Huey/Corbis; 46 (TR) ©Thomas & Pat Leeson/Photo Researchers, Inc., (CR) ©John Burcham/National Geographic Image Collection; 47 (TL) Getty Images, (TR) ©Mark Karrass/Corbis; 48 (CL) ©Frans Lanting/Corbis, (BL) ©Bill Ross/Corbis, (C) ©Jeff Hunter/ Photographer's Choice RR/Getty Images; 49 Mike Dunning/©DK Images; 50 (BR) ©National Geographic/Getty Images, (TR) ©George D. Lepp/Corbis; 51 (TL) ©Peter Lilja/The Image Bank/Getty Images, (TR) ©David Kjaer/Nature Picture Library; 52 (BL) ©Marc Moritsch/National Geographic Image Collection, (BR) ©Richard I'Anson/Lonely Planet Images, (TR) ©J. A. Kraulis/Masterfile Corporation; 53 (TL) ©Cosmo Condina/Getty Images, (TR) ©Tim Fitzharris/Getty Images; 55 ©Image Source Limited, ©Brooks Kraft/Corbis; 56 (TL) ©S. Carmona/Corbis, (CL) Getty Images, (C) ©Thomas Northcut/Riser/Getty Images; 57 Getty Images; 58 ©George S. de Blonsky/Alamy Images; 59 (TR) Getty Images, (BC) ©Louis Fox/Stone/Getty Images; 60 (TR) ©Kevin Horan/Getty Images, (CR) ©Donald Miralle/Taxi/Getty Images; 61 (TR) ©Terry Vine/Getty Images, (TL) Getty Images; 62 (TL) ©W. Perry Conway/Corbis, (CL) Animals Animals/Earth Scenes, (CL) ©Nicolas Russell/Photographer's Choice/Getty Images, (C) ©Marcos Brindicci/Corbis; 63 (CR) Gordon Clayton/©DK Images, (CR) Geoff Brightling/©DK Images; 64 (TR) ©Steve Smith/Photographer's Choice/Getty Images, (C) ©Derek Bromhall/OSF/Animals Animals/Earth Scenes; 64 ©Chris Jones/Corbis; 65 ©Nancy Rotenberg/Animals Animals/Earth Scenes; 66 (TR) ©David Stoecklein/Corbis, (CR) ©W. Perry Conway/Corbis; 67 (TL) ©Rachel Epstein/PhotoEdit, (TR) ©ONOKY/Getty Images; 68 (TL) ©Tony Freeman/PhotoEdit, (CL) Jupiter Images, (C) ©moodboard/Corbis; 69 Stockdisc, ©Ableimages/Riser/Getty Images; 71 (TR) ©MM Productions/Corbis/Jupiter Images, (BR) Corbis; 72 (TL) ©Gerard Lacz/Animals Animals/Earth Scenes, (TL) ©Paul Bricknell/Dorling Kindersley/Getty Images, (CL) Getty Images, (CL) ©WoodyStock/Alamy Images, (CL) Zia Soleil/Iconica/Getty Images; 73 ©Mike Brinson/Getty Images; 74 (TL) ©Altrendo Images/Getty Images, (CL) ©Felix Clouzot/Getty Image, (C) ©Mark Richards/PhotoEdit; 75 Getty Images; 76 (TR) ©William B. Plowman/Stringer/Getty Images, (B) ©Peter Cavanagh/Alamy Images; 77 ©David McNew/Getty Images; 78 (TR) ©Jeff Greenberg/PhotoEdit, (CR) ©Purestock/Alamy; 79 David Cruz/U.S.AL DIA/©NewsCom; 81 (C) ©Visions of America/Alamy Images, (TL) ©Joseph Sohm/Corbis; 82 (TR) ©Wally McNamee/Corbis, (CR) ©DreamPictures/Getty Images; 83 (TR) ©Martin Athenstaedt/dpa/Corbis, (CR) ©Bettmann/Corbis; 84 Will & Deni McIntyre/Corbis; 85 (TR) ©Rich Krauss/Corbis, (TR) ©Blend Images/Alamy; 87 (TL) ©Jon Arnold Images/Alamy Images, (C) Getty Images; 88 (C) ©Sean Justice/ Iconica/Getty Images, (TR) Getty Images; 90 (TC) ©Purestock/SuperStock, (BR) Getty Images, (TR) ©Woody Wooden/SuperStock; 91 ©Steve Vidler/SuperStock; 92 (TR) ©Craig Tuttle/Corbis, (CR) ©Zia Soleil/Iconica/Getty Images, (CL) ©age fotostock/SuperStock; 93 (TL) ©Hans Reinhard/Corbis, (TR) ©Scott Tysick/Masterfile Corporation; 94 (C,T) Getty Images, (TL) ©Tim Davis/Corbis, (CL) ©age fotostock/SuperStock; 95 ©Gallo Images Roots RF collection/Getty Images; 96 (TR) ©Tom Walker/Photographer's Choice/Getty Images, (CR) ©Corbis Premium RF/Alamy, (BR) ©Jim Zuckerman/Corbis; 97 ©Didier Robcis/Corbis; 98 (TR) ©Wulf Pfeiffer/epa/Corbis, (CR) ©Buddy Mays/Corbis; 99 (TL) Animals Animals/Earth Scenes, (C) ©Joel Sartore/National Geographic Image Collection; 100 (TL) ©Mark A. Johnson/Corbis, (CL) ©Jerry Kobalenko/The Image Bank/Getty Images, (C) Corbis; 101 ©Werner Forman/Art Resource, NY; 102 (TR) ©Cosmo Condina/Mira, (CR) ©Craig Tuttle/Corbis; 103 (CR) ©Terry W. Eggers/Corbis, (CR) ©Mike Brinson/The Image Bank/Getty Images; 104 (CL) ©Arthur Morris/Corbis, (CR) ©Datacraft/AGE Fotostock; 105 ©Joel Satore/Getty Images; 106 (TL) ©Reuters/Corbis, (CL) Jupiter Images, (CL) ©Gene Blevins /Corbis; 108 (TR) ©Scott Stulberg/Corbis, (CL) ©Jim Reed/Corbis, (CR) ©Anthony Redpath/Corbis; 110 (TR) ©A. T. Willett/The Image Bank/Getty Images, (CL) ©John Sevigny/Corbis, (CR) ©Reuters/Corbis; 111 ©Stephen St. John/National Geographic Image Collection; 112 (TL) ©Corbis Premium RF/Alamy, (C) DLILLC/Corbis, (CL) ©Darrell Gulin/Corbis; 113 Geoff Brightling/©DK Images; 114 (CR) ©Alan R. Moller/Stone/Getty Images, (TC) ©Réunion des Musées Nationaux/Art Resource, NY; 115 ©Barry Lewis/Corbis; 116 (TR, CR) ©Jeff Vanuga/Corbis, (CR) ©James L. Amos/Corbis; 117 ©Ursula Gahwiler/Corbis; 119 ©AFP/Getty Images, Jupiter Images, ©Koopman/Corbis, ©Myrleen Ferguson Cate/PhotoEdit, ©Corbis/Jupiter Images; 120 (TL) ©Dirk Anschutz/ Stone/Getty Images, (TL) Getty Image, (C) ©FPG/Staff/Hulton Archive/Getty Images; 121 (BR) B. Bird/zefa/Corbis, (TR) ©DK Images, (TL) Comstock Inc., (BL) ©IPS Co, Ltd./Beatworks/Corbis; 123 (TR) ©George Disario/Corbis, (BR) Corbis; 124 ©Corbis/Jupiter Images; 125 (TL) ©Darby Sawchuk/Alamy Images, (TR) ©Massimo Borchi/Corbis; 126 (TL) ©Purestock/Jupiter Images, (C) ©Doug Allen and Sue Flood/The Image Bank/Getty Images, (TL) ©John Warden/SuperStock; 127 (TR) ©Art Wolfe/Stone/Getty Images, (BR) ©Herbert Spichtinger/zefa/Corbis; 128 (CR) ©Jupiterimages/Creatas/Alamy, (BC) ©Joe Vogan/SuperStock, (TR) Veer, Inc.; 129 (BR) ©Yusuf Ahmad/Reuters/Corbis, (BC) ©Winston Luzier/Transtock/Corbis, (BL) ©Corbis/Jupiter Images; 130 (TR) ©Picture Partners/Alamy Images, (C) Punchstock; 131 ©Roy Toft/National Geographic Image Collection; 132 (TL) ©Jupiterimages/Creatas/Alamy, (C) ©Bettmann/Corbis; 133 ©Corbis RF/Alamy; 134 (CR) Art Resource, NY, (TR) ©The Jacob and Gwendolyn Lawrence Foundation/Art Resource, NY; 135 ©Tamara Reynolds/Corbis; 136 ©Piotr Powietrzynski/Photographer's Choice/Getty Images; 137 Corbis; 138 (TL) ©Robin Lynne Gibson/Photographer's Choice/Getty Images, (C) ©The Gallery Collection/Corbis; 139 (C) ©Archivo Iconografico, S.A./Corbis, (TR) ©Emmanuel Faure/Getty Images; 141 ©Roy King/SuperStock; 142 (TR) ©PhotoSpin, Inc./Alamy, (CR) Art Resource, NY; 144 (TR) ©Tim McConville/zefa/Corbis, (TL) ©Corbis Premium RF/Alamy, (C) Getty Images; 145 ©simple stock shots/Punchstock; 146 (TR) ©Royalty-Free/Corbis, (BR) ©H. Armstrong Roberts/Corbis, (CR) ©RubberBall/Alamy; 147 (TR) ©Sharon Montrose/The Image Bank/Getty Images; 149 (TL) ©Jim Craigmyle/Corbis, (TR) ©Jupiterimages/Comstock Premium/Alamy; 151 Getty Images, ©Marcel Antonisse/epa/Corbis, Jupiter Images, MSFC/NASA; 152 ©Gerolf Kalt/zefa/Corbis, ©David R. Frazier Photolibrary, Inc./Alamy Images; 154 ©Jim Zuckerman/Corbis, (CR) ©Ronnie Kaufman/Corbis, (TR) Jupiter Images; 155 (TR) ©Corbis/Jupiter Images, (C) ©Mike Powell/Getty Images; 156 ©Marko Georgiev/Getty Images; 158 (TL) ©Kenneth Garrett/Woodfin Camp/Contributor/Getty Images, (TR) ©Larry Dale Godon/zefa/Corbis, (C) SuperStock; 159 ©Bettmann/Corbis; 160 (TL) ©Stephen Alvarez/National Geographic Image Collection, (TR) ©Keith Dannemiller/D70s/Corbis, (BR) ©Historical Picture Archive/Corbis; 162 (TL, TR) Jupiter Images; 162 ©Wolfgang Weinhaupl/Jupiter Images; 164 (TL) Clive Streeter/©DK Images, (CL) ©Jeff Foott/Corbis, (C) ©John Kelly/The Image Bank/Getty Images, (TR) ©Rubberball/Jupiter Images; 165 ©SuperStock/Alamy, (TR) Stefan Schuetz/zefa/Corbis; 166 (TC) Getty Images, (BR) Jupiter Images; 168 (CL) ©Blend Images/Jupiter Images, (CR) ©Vince Streano/Getty Images; 170 (C, TL) Steve Morgan/©NewsCom, (C) Antonio Mo/Getty Images; 171 Jupiter Images; 172 (TR) Demetrio Carrasco/©DK Images, (CR) NASA; 173 Jupiter Images; 174 (CL) ©Per Eriksson/Getty Images, (CR) ©Jenny E. Ross/Corbis; 176 ©NASA/Roger Ressmeyer/Corbis, ©Deco Images/Alamy, ©World Perspectives/Getty Images; 177 JSC/NASA; 178 (TR) ©Ross M. Horowitz/Getty Images, (TR) NASA; 180 NASA; 183 ©Bettmann/Corbis; 184 (TL) Getty Images, (TL) ©Jupiterimages/Thinkstock/Alamy, (C) Corbis; 186 (TR) Getty Images, (BC) ©Christine Kokot/dpa/Corbis; 187 ©Bettmann/Corbis; 188 (TR) ©Tom Stewart/Corbis, (B) ©B2M Productions/Getty Images; 190 (TL) ©Creasource/Corbis, (CL) ©David Arky/Corbis, (C) ©Mark Kauffman/Stringer/Getty Images; 192 (T) ©Duomo/Corbis, (BR) ©Michael Wong/Corbis; 193 (TR) ©Corbis Premium RF/Alamy, (TR) ©Jeff Greenberg/PhotoEdit; 194 (CL) ©Erich Lessing/Art Resource, NY, (TR) ©epa/Corbis, (CR) Getty Images; 196 (TL) ©Johner/Getty Images, (C) ©Farinaz Taghavi/Corbis; 197 ©Dorling Kindersley/Getty Images, ©Jupiterimages/Comstock Images/Alamy; 198 (CR) ©Corbis/Jupiter Images, (BR) ©Pilar Olivares/Reuters/Corbis; 200 (TR) ©Joseph De Leo/Getty Image, (BR) ©Ian Shaw/Alamy Images; 202 (TL) ©David Madison/Corbis, (CL) ©Erik Snyder/Getty Image, (C) ©moodboard/Corbis; 203 (TC) ©Wolfgang Deuter/zefa/Corbis, (TR) ©Image Source; 204 (TR) ©Don Emmert/AFP/Getty Images, (BR) ©Corbis Premium RF/Alamy; 205 ©David L. Moor/Alamy Images; 206 (TR) ©David Young-Wolff/PhotoEdit, (CL) ©Duomo/Corbis, (BR) Getty Images; 208 (TL) ©Ernie Walker/NASA, (CL, C) NASA; 210 NASA; 212 (CR) ©Neo Vision/Getty Images, (CL) ©Reven T.C. Wurman/Alamy; 213 ©Richard T. Nowitz/Corbis.

Antonyms

Base Words/Root Words

Context Clues

Dictionary

Multiple-Meaning Words

Prefixes

Suffixes

Synonyms

Thesaurus

Word Families

Word Origins: Roots

A Vocabulary Handbook

Antonyms

An antonym is a word that has the opposite meaning of another word. *Day* is an antonym for *night*.

Day

Night

Antonym = Opposite

Strategy for Antonyms

1. Identify the word for which you want to find an antonym.
2. Think of other words or phrases that have the opposite meaning.
3. Use a thesaurus to help you find antonyms.
4. Use a dictionary to check the antonyms' meanings, so that you use the words that best communicate your ideas.

Synonyms

A synonym is a word that has almost the same meaning as another word. *Hot* is a synonym for *scorching.*

Synonym = Same

Strategy for Synonyms

1. Identify the word for which you want to find a synonym.
2. Think of other words or phrases that have the same, or almost the same, meaning.
3. Use a thesaurus to help you find more synonyms, and make a list.
4. Use a dictionary to find the word that best communicates your ideas.

Base Words/Root Words

A base word, also called a root word, is a word that can't be broken into smaller words. *Friend* is a root of *friendly* and *friendship*.

Earth

Unearthly

Earth is the base word.

Strategy for Base Words

1. Look for a base word in the unknown word.
2. Determine the meaning of the base word.
3. Guess the meaning of the unfamiliar word. Does it make sense in the sentence?
4. Check the meaning in a dictionary.

Prefixes

A prefix is a word part added to the beginning of a base word to form a new word.

Wrap

Unwrap

Strategy for Prefixes

1. Look at the unknown word and identify the prefix.
2. What does the base word mean? If you're not sure, check the dictionary.
3. Use what you know about the base word and the prefix to figure out the meaning of the unknown word.
4. Use a dictionary to check your guess.

Common Prefixes and Their Meanings

un–	not
re–	again, back
in–	not
dis–	not, opposite of
pre–	before

Suffixes

A suffix is a word part added to the end of a base word to form a new word.

Shoe

Shoeless

Common Suffixes and Their Meanings

-ly	characteristic of
-tion	act, process
-able	can be done
-ment	action or process
-less	without

Strategy for Suffixes

1. Look at the unknown word and identify the suffix.
2. What does the base word mean? If you're not sure, check a dictionary.
3. Use what you know about the base word and the suffix to figure out the meaning of the unknown word.
4. Use a dictionary to check your guess.

Context Clues

Context clues are the words and sentences found around an unknown word that can help you understand a word's meaning. Use context clues to figure out what a fireworm is.

I can't decide whether to write my underwater-creature report on a starfish, a dolphin, a fireworm, or an octopus.

Strategy for Context Clues

1. Look for clues in the words and phrases around the unknown word.
2. Take a guess at the word's meaning. Does it make sense in the sentence?
3. Use a dictionary to check your guess.

Word Families

Word families are related words that all have the same base word.

Cycle

Bicycle

Cyclist

Strategy for Word Families

1. Find the base word in your unknown word.
2. Identify the meaning of the base word.
3. Guess the meaning of the unfamiliar word. Does it make sense in the sentence?
4. Use a dictionary to check your guess.

Word Origins: Roots

Many English words contain Greek and Latin roots.

Telephone

Dentures

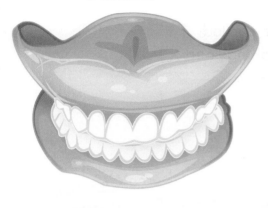

Tractor

Latin Roots

dent	tooth
dict	to say; to speak
scrib	to write
sub	under; below
tract	to pull
vis	to see

Greek Roots

auto	self
bio	life
micro	very small
ology	the study of
phon	sound; voice
scope	see
tele	far

Strategy for Roots

1. Use what you know about Greek and Latin roots to guess the meaning of the unknown word.
2. Does your guess make sense in the sentence?
3. Use a dictionary to check your guess.

Multiple-Meaning Words

Multiple-meaning words are words that have different meanings depending on how they are used. Homonyms, homographs, and homophones are all multiple-meaning words.

Homographs

Homographs are words that are spelled the same but have different meanings and sometimes different pronunciations.

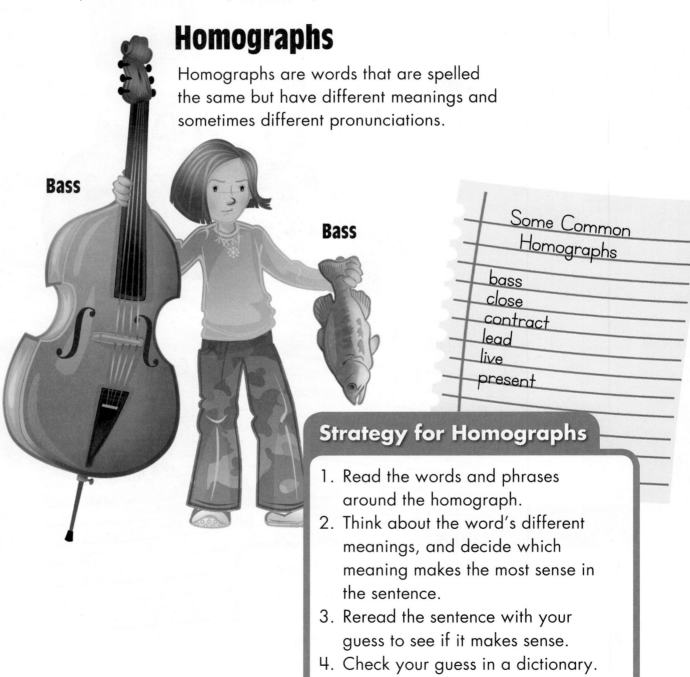

Bass

Bass

Some Common Homographs

bass
close
contract
lead
live
present

Strategy for Homographs

1. Read the words and phrases around the homograph.
2. Think about the word's different meanings, and decide which meaning makes the most sense in the sentence.
3. Reread the sentence with your guess to see if it makes sense.
4. Check your guess in a dictionary.

Homonyms

Homonyms are words that are pronounced the same and have the same spelling, but their meanings are different.

Squash

Squash

Some Common Homonyms

pen
duck
mail
ear
bank
bark

Strategy for Homonyms

1. Read the words and phrases near the homonym.
2. Think about the word's different meanings, and decide which one makes the most sense.
3. Reread the sentence with your guess to see if it makes sense.
4. Use a dictionary to check your guess.

Homophones

Homophones are words that are pronounced the same way but have different spellings and different meanings.

Ball

Bawl

Some Common Homophones

ate	eight
bored	board
brake	break
knight	night
weight	wait

Strategy for Homophones

1. Think about the different spellings and meanings of homophones.
2. Check a dictionary for definitions of the words.
3. Use the word that best fits your writing.

Dictionary

A dictionary is a reference book that lists words alphabetically.
It can be used to look up definitions, parts of speech, spelling,
and other forms of words.

punc·tu·al ❶ (pungk′ chü əl), ❷ ADJECTIVE.
❸ prompt; exactly on time: ❹ *He is always punctual.*
❺ **punc′tu·al·ly** ADVERB.

Strategy for Dictionary

1. Identify the unknown word.
2. Look up the word in a dictionary. Entries are listed alphabetically.
3. Find the part of the entry that has the information you are looking for.
4. Use the diagram above as a guide to help you locate the information you want.

❶ Pronunciation

❷ Part of speech

❸ Definitions

❹ Example sentence

❺ Other form of the word and its part of speech

Thesaurus

A thesaurus is a book of synonyms. Sometimes it will also contain antonyms. Look through the synonyms to find one with the best meaning by using a dictionary.

cute

adjective

attractive, appealing, amusing, charming, adorable, enchanting.

ANTONYMS: ugly, dull, unappealing

Strategy for Thesaurus

1. Look up the word in a thesaurus. Entries are listed alphabetically.
2. Locate the synonyms for your word.
3. Find the word with the exact meaning you want.